MANAGING EFFORT
GETTING RESULTS

A COACHING SYSTEM FOR MANAGERS

MANAGING EFFORT GETTING RESULTS

A COACHING SYSTEM FOR MANAGERS

John C. Marshall, Ph.D.
Bob McHardy, CLU

National Library of Canada Cataloguing in Publication

Marshall, John C.

Managing Effort, Getting Results: A Coaching System For
Managers
John Charles Marshall, Robert J. McHardy

ISBN 0-9682287-4-7

1.   Management.
2.   Managers-Training of. I. Marshall, John C., Ph.D. II. Title.

HD31.M233 2003   658   C2003-902885-2

Table of Contents

Foreword

About the Authors

John C. Marshall, Chairman of the Self Management Group, has a Ph.D. in psychology from York University. His doctoral thesis, The Competitive Environment: Effects and Influences, drew on both academic and experiential sources as a former professional hockey player and as a hockey coach at York University and in Italy, John is well-versed in the psychology of competition and performance. His academic interests in statistics and computer modeling led to his work in developing several profiling and selection systems: the Predictor Of Performance (POP™), the Management Potential POP™ (MPP™), the LeaderPOP™, the Quality Service POP™, the TrustPOP™, Integrity POP™ Fluid Intelligence, EQ, Cognitive Skills and Diversity and Inclusion.

As a consultant with the Self Management Group, John has an enviable track record in success coaching for groups that range from professional athletes, teachers, and coaches to senior executives. In a variety of unique programs and seminars, he deals with many aspects of attitude management, motivation, team building, and building success habits. He has also written, and contributed to a number of books and articles on organizational growth, training, and competition in sports and business.

Bob McHardy, is the former president of the PLUS Corporation, and a former principal of the Self Management Group. He is an accomplished public speaker, management trainer, sales trainer, and executive coach. Bob helped build the PLUS Corporation into a major training organization that works with some of North America's largest banks, insurance companies, pharmaceuticals, retail, and automobile companies. Popular seminars and training programs that focus on the distinctive "Managing Effort" system and on the development of self-managing employees (pioneered by the PLUS Corporation) have earned him the respect of his colleagues, and made the concept of "self-management" an industry benchmark.

About the Self Management Group

The Self Management Group is a world leader in Screening, Selecting, Developing and Retaining Top Performers. SMG is the home of the POP™ and has become one of the largest assessment companies operating in 40 countries and 40 languages. Proprietary assessments, unique self management training, extensive global cloud database, corporate diagnostics and the introduction of artificial intelligence and bot technology help our clients continue to utilize the latest in talent management solutions.

POP™ (Predictor Of Performance)
- #1 Sales Assessment Company
- 40 years in business
- 40+ Countries
- 40+ Languages
- 3500+ Clients

Acknowledgements

This book is dedicated to all the Self Managers and Golden Eagles who have helped us understand the power of self-management. We thank the many people who contributed to its development and its final form. A special mention to Ian Perrin, who took a risk in leaving his management role with a large Canadian bank to join Self Management Group. For over 25 years now, Ian has made an enormous contribution to the success of the Managing Effort seminars, introducing them to new industries, to government services, and to several international clients. His initiatives and his input to program content have made the PLUS Corporation a leading training organization.

Thanks as well to the thousands of people who have participated in our workshops and seminars over the last four decades. The experiences they have shared with us have helped to clarify our principles and have suggested many practical strategies for self-management and coaching high performance.

THERE IS ONLY ONE WAY TO

GET FROM OBJECTIVES TO RESULTS:

EFFORT.

Preface

MANAGING EFFORT—AND GETTING RESULTS

The Effort Grid

The grid set out below represents four possible combinations of talent and effort that your employees (or sales reps, workers, or team members—anyone whose performance you will be held accountable for) may exhibit.

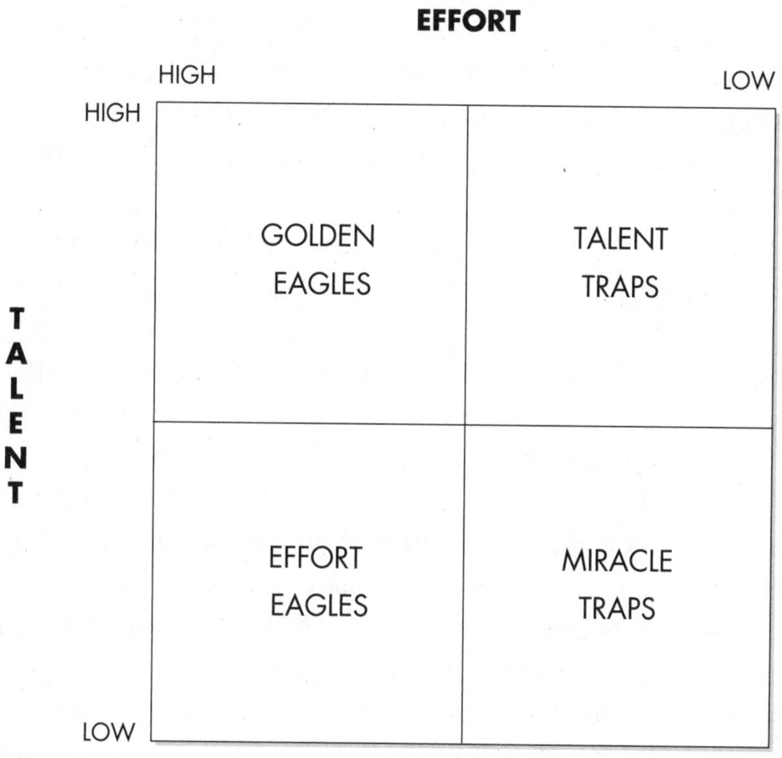

EFFORT

	HIGH	LOW
HIGH	GOLDEN EAGLES	TALENT TRAPS
LOW	EFFORT EAGLES	MIRACLE TRAPS

(Vertical axis label: **T A L E N T**)

The Effort Grid

This grid helps managers and executives to identify the full range of performers in a workplace. The grid accounts for what everyone already knows about their people—that there are some real assets. Those high-talent, high-effort people—the golden eagles—typically get the best results, and get them consistently. And of course there are a few liabilities: low-talent, low-effort individuals, the miracle traps who only get satisfactory results by a miracle. The grid also highlights two important categories that managers who focus exclusively on results might overlook: effort eagles and talent traps.

Actually, many managers spend a great deal of time thinking about talent traps—high-talent but low-effort employees. Some of this time, as we will argue, could be used more productively. A talent trap often appears to be a problem worth working on. Talent is obviously valuable, and it's easy to associate with success. As a result, managers tend to give talent traps a lot of support, a lot of second chances, and a lot of opportunities to put those talents to work. But without *effort*, those opportunities are wasted.

And it is the effort eagles—people who consistently and energetically expend effort, even though they may be less skilled or lack some specific talent—who actually can make the most of such opportunities, especially with the support of resources, training, and development. This has led us to argue for some deep reorientations of *managerial* effort.

"The Results Grid" shows the results typically associated with these four categories. Once again, the high and low ends of the scale are predictable: it's no surprise that golden eagles get the most results and that miracle traps get the least. But when managers use the effort grid to analyze their teams, they often discover that they have been spending most of their time and energy on the people who *aren't* getting the necessary results while neglecting the people who, one way or another, *are* meeting quotas, building business, and hitting goals. For these managers, talent traps and miracle traps are the main challenge of management, a challenge they feel they must address.

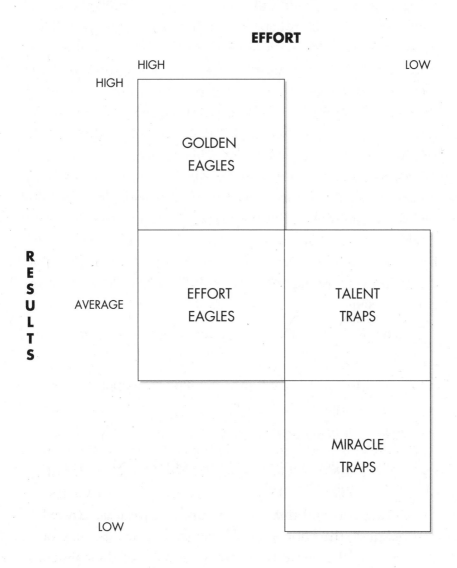

EFFORT

The Results Grid

In reacting to a perceived problem, managers sometimes lose sight of the *satisfactions* of management. Think about your own team. Do some of your people show high levels of effort and achieve excellent results? Do some make the effort, even if they don't quite get the results they deserve? If you think about it for a moment, you will probably agree that they are the people you most enjoy working with—even if you don't spend the most time with them. They are the most productive, they probably welcome your support, and they provide the best return on your investment of time and energy. Your greatest job satisfaction likely comes from seeing them do well, seeing them get the results that they need and achieve their goals.

Imagine, then, what it would be like if *all* your people were golden eagles and effort eagles! It's not impossible. This book will show you how to get *improved results* by developing and retaining "eagles." It outlines a practical management system based on *coaching* your best and your most promising people. It also provides some answers to the key questions managers ask. For example

- What is the best way to hold my people responsible and accountable for their actions and results?

- How can I develop and retain a high-effort person who is not getting good results?

- How do I deal with a high-talent, poor-effort employee?

- How do I determine the amount of time and effort to spend on an employee?

- Where do I spend my time and energy to achieve the greatest return?

MANAGERS ARE MEASURED BY RESULTS—RESULTS THAT COME FROM OTHER PEOPLE'S PERFORMANCE

Introduction

THE CHALLENGES OF MANAGEMENT

What's So Hard About Management?

As consultants, we have worked with thousands of managers. As a group, they are hard-working, committed, thoughtful, and responsible people. And the more we listen to their discussions—of typical problems, creative solutions, recurrent challenges—the clearer it becomes that managers do some of the hardest work there is.

Managers all face the same essential challenge. They are *responsible* for getting results, and they are held responsible for their team's or department's results, but they cannot *control* those results. They are *measured* by results—the results that *other people* get. It often takes some time for managers—especially if they have come to management from production, sales, or customer service—to get used to the special nature of managerial accountability. That is, while they are *organizationally* accountable for their department's results, they are not *personally* responsible for the results each individual employee achieves. It isn't the manager who produces the units, makes the sales, or deals with the customers—but it's typically the manager who has to see that it is done.

A manager must also be aware of the relationship between the wide-scale or long-term objectives of the organization and the narrow range of circumstances that he or she deals with directly on a day-to-day basis. This relationship follows from the distinction between an organization's "managers" and its "executives." Executives are oriented towards "the big picture," towards long-range strategies and industry-level decisions.

Managers, however, deal with the hands-on, day-to-day application of those strategies and decisions, mediating between the executives and the employees. An analogy may be useful: managers are like the coaches of a sports team; executives are like general managers. They have the same objectives, but they operate in different spheres, using different skills and procedures.

Burn-out: Misplaced Effort

Managers face the challenges of a complex kind of responsibility—one which makes them particularly vulnerable to burn-out. Faced with a difference between the results they must report at the end of the week, month, or quarter and the results their people are actually producing, some managers respond by overextending themselves in an attempt to anticipate more, control more, and do more than a single person really can do. This extra investment of time and energy may eventually lead to burnout—the feeling that one's returns are significantly less than one's investment of time and energy.

Actually, managers don't burn out because they are trying to do "too much" in their jobs. The problem is that their effort is *misplaced:* they burn out because they are trying to do *everyone's* jobs—to the point of taking responsibility for everything. If productivity falls, for instance, or if sales taper off, it's *not* the manager's job to go back to the shop floor or start making sales calls. But many managers, especially those who became managers because of their high productivity, or their good track record in sales, or their expertise in specific roles, find it hard to adapt to, and stay with, a management role.

What Can Managers Manage?

Some managers, when they start to chase results, stop being

managers, stop doing their proper job. So what is this job?

A good manager knows that the real challenge of management isn't to do it all by yourself, but to get people to take responsibility for their own efforts and effectiveness. The core of our approach is the belief that managers work best when they manage *effort*. Given the title of this book, this must come as no surprise. But people are sometimes surprised by the main corollary of this belief: that most of the time spent attempting to control results is *time wasted*. You can, however, manage effort. And when managing effort, you can *influence* results, often substantially. Since you cannot control results *completely* or *directly*, managing by results is problematic, if not impossible. Managing by results is always "too late": results have always *already* happened, and they can't be changed. You can celebrate (when they're good) or agonize (when they're bad), but the results are history.

Coaching Effort—The Central Concept

This book describes a practical, day-to-day system that helps managers manage, rather than try to take over the functions and duties of the people they oversee. This system is centered on the concept of *coaching:* the manager's functions and roles are defined, precisely and practically, in terms of coaching effort to get results. Using the principles of this coaching system, you can develop strictly *managerial* objectives, distinct from sales targets, growth projections, or organizational goals, which will allow you to develop and achieve significant *managerial* growth.

Our coaching program is based on lessons learned in business and on psychological principles and research. It integrates the habits and behaviors of the best coaches, in business and other contexts, and draws on research to account for their success.

Unlike some researchers, we are not solely concerned with "best practices"—a set of routines or procedures that can simply be adopted by others. Everyone's best practices—including your own!—are developed in specific contexts, from which they can seldom be detached. We are more concerned to look *behind* what managers (including you) are doing right, to understand why it works—and to show how that success can be replicated.

As a system, the "managing effort" approach sets out a number of principles that govern behavior and ensure a high level of consistency and predictability. There is plenty of room for personal variations and situational differences; we don't expect every manager to have the same style or to deal with the same circumstances. And it is an open system. It easily incorporates existing skills, abilities, and knowledge, but does not make them the status quo; there is always room for more and better talent and effort. Finally, as a practical system, our approach also focuses on applications—specific, *practical*, effective procedures that will help you allocate your managerial resources, energy, and time for better productivity, performance, and results.

Building on Strengths

This coaching program *does not replace anything that already exists.* It is an adaptive, evolutionary approach that will allow you to capitalize on what you already know. Because it is a management system, it provides a basis for decision-making, a system that can be applied immediately to the resources, procedures, and circumstances that you have in place. Some management systems (according to their proponents) sound very attractive, but they often require you to change things completely—yourself or your circumstances, or both. Our coaching program, in contrast, encourages you to identify and build on existing strengths. It offers a more pragmatic approach to the challenges of management. To use the system, you don't have to change who you are. You may decide, however, to change the way you do some things. The crucial shift will be to do the things you do most successfully more often and more consistently.

Rather than demanding a complete overhaul of your workplace, your staff, or your style, this coaching system works "from the inside out." Some management programs only provide new ways of doing the same old things. For instance, they may emphasize techniques, routines, and practical procedures (time-management systems, project or campaign planners, reporting systems, etc.). Sometimes, these recommendations are based on a literal application of observed "best practices": "If filling out daily quality control worksheets works for them, it will work for you too!" Overhauling procedures can indeed introduce economies and increase efficiency. But no amount of tinkering with externals will genuinely resolve issues of motivation, effort, and performance in the workplace. This coaching system allows you, instead, to tap each individual's potential for success, and to help your people become maintenance-free self-managers.

This coaching system also encourages you to build on your own strengths. You probably do many things very well already. In fact, you might be surprised to know just how much you can do. People aren't always *aware* of their competence: they take for granted certain skills or abilities. The coaching program will reinforce and *increase* "conscious competence." Of course, you could do this on your own. Any successful manager has learned how to apply effective strategies on a consistent basis. But this book will shorten the learning curve, helping you to identify what you do well and to recognize what you can improve—and offering new opportunities for your own personal and professional growth.

"No More Problems"

One of the perennial challenges of management is to keep focusing proactively on *opportunities* in addition to responding to *problems*. The difference doesn't really depend on circumstances, but on attitude. Interpreting a situation as a "problem" in need of a "solution" often seems the only way to "get things right." There's nothing wrong with doing things right, but not every success consists in overcoming some problematic obstacle. When managers (and management programs) focus exclusively on problems, it is easy to overlook many positive achievements and the people responsible for them. Managers who find themselves spending a lot of time putting out fires will eventually find that they are doing nothing else. If you turn up for work every day wearing a firefighter's helmet, people are going to start to think that the only way to get your attention is to shout "Fire!"

The coaching system takes the emphasis off "problems" and places it on opportunities and strengths. Of course, it would be naive to suggest that you don't have to deal with problems. But is that *all* you ought to be doing? The system, since it is centered on developing the potential for success, redefines "problems" as *opportunities* for action and for growth. Take what are often referred to as "motivation" or "performance" issues, for example. These are often expressed in *negative* terms—for example, as a "problem with poor morale" or as a "failure to communicate incentive." The use of such terms implies that something has already gone wrong and that now it can only be mitigated or minimized. A manager's options seem to be restricted to various forms of damage control—the response of a manager who spends more time reacting to results and problems than coaching effort.

The managing effort system, by contrast, treats such issues in terms of what is *going to be done,* not just in terms of what has already happened. Coaching is proactive as well as reactive; it evaluates results, whether good or bad, but directs attention to the progress that can be made on that basis. Coaching also pays more attention to the strong performers who, conventionally, may not attract a manager's notice, simply because they are getting the job done—they don't present any "problem." Managerial coaches support the best efforts of their best employees. When you recognize the strengths that your people exhibit, you can begin to *lead* your team, rather than following along behind to clean up the mess.

Quality and Quantity

The managing effort system distinguishes and balances *performance* and *results,* and focuses on the quality and the quantity of *effort.* This kind of analysis is crucial. An "average performer" may be making a very strong effort, but not very often; alternatively, he or she may be trying all the time, but not very hard. In either case, the results may be about the same, but the associated performance issues demand quite different responses. The quality of the effort, which is a matter of skills and attitudes, must be distinguished from the quantity of the effort, which is determined by the level and intensity of behavior. Considering such essential determinants of performance produces more precise evaluations and more accurate insights into people's potential for development. Good coaches are able to balance effort and results. Managers who restrict their attention to results alone often discount the amount of effort made by so-called "underperformers" (who may in fact be only *under-*

achievers). And this may lead the manager to seriously underestimate an employee's potential for good results. A manager's principal challenge is to encourage people to work hard to get results—and simply to *work hard consistently*. Top performers try hard and try consistently. People who show these high levels of effort ought to be appreciated for their performance and coached, developed, and trained to achieve results. That's the coach's job: to help turn effort into results.

Coaching and the Effort Grid

The managing effort system is evolutionary, building on and improving what is already in place. Neither you nor your employees have to change radically. There are strategies for any set of circumstances and for even the most intractable categories of so-called "problem employees." By distinguishing genuine, productive coaching from exhausting, futile *coaxing*, you will learn how to develop and retain golden eagles (high-effort, high-ability performers) and effort eagles (high-effort, low-ability employees). You will also learn how, by distinguishing external reinforcement and internal motivation (and the related concepts of compliance and commitment), you can coach talent traps (low-effort, high-ability employees) and even some miracle traps (low-effort, low-ability people) to make commitments and *choose* to succeed. These coaching strategies will, in turn, maximize the returns on your own investments of time and effort, enhancing your own professional and personal satisfaction.

As an evolutionary process, this coaching system is also *continuous*. It is designed to discover opportunities and open up ways to move forward. It offers not a destination but a horizon, towards which you can continually advance. There is no point at which you can be said to be "finished"; no limits are set to the improvement and the growth, both organizational and individual, that it offers.

Developing Self-Managers

The managing effort system provides a practical approach that you can use every day to build on strengths and to create *self-managers*—employees who don't need to be "managed" in the ordinary sense. That is, they need less direct supervision and fewer explicit instructions. Perhaps most importantly, they seldom create "problems" that a manager is compelled to "solve." Instead, managers can become their consultants or facilitators. Confident, effective, and well-organized, self-managers are typically a manager's best performers and display consistently high levels of effort. They take responsibility for their behavior and their careers, acting on their own authority to make decisions and to make—and keep—commitments.

Self-managers establish priorities and use their resources efficiently. Like any good manager, self-managers capitalize on their abilities. As we will explain, they "control the controllables." Consequently, they are very clear about their strengths and weaknesses. Since they are always careful to continue to do what they are good at doing, self-managers are capable of impressive performance and results. It's not that they are superhuman; they simply make the most of their advantages, while reducing their exposure to areas in which they still need to develop abilities.

Because they appraise themselves realistically, self-managers are ready to address their needs and seek the training and development they require. Self-managers typically seek challenges, both in their careers and in their personal growth, and because they are efficient, they have the time and energy to devote to new initiatives and activities.

Benefits of Developing Self-Managers

The personal and professional benefits of developing self-managers are plain. Working with self-managers gives you more time, more independence, and less stress. As one coaching manager put it, "I'm having a better time on the job—and better vacations too!" Self-managers don't constantly need a boss to tell them what to do, or a supervisor hovering at their side. They can be trusted to carry out the commitments they make. When they need a coach or a consultant, they know it, and come looking for you. And you will have the time to provide the sort of solid, direct assistance they require.

A team made up of high-performing self-managers *challenges* you to coach them. You will enjoy increased productivity—and not only the quantity but the quality of results will improve. Managers enjoy closer, more productive relationships with self-managing employees, since both are focused on successful achievements and positive potential. It becomes easier to share a sense of accomplishment and pride, to recognize each individual's contributions, and even, when necessary, to negatively reinforce or to extinguish poor effort and performance.

Reconditioning

The managing effort system is based on essential principles that many people already know and that most people accept without question. The benefits of developing self-managers seem to be self-evident. So why is it necessary to set out a coaching program? Why isn't everyone doing it already?

The answer has to do with some old and very well-established habits, habits that appear not only in business but in society at large. Our culture sets a high value on individual responsibility, initiative, and effort—the characteristic qualities of a good self-manager. But at the same time, most of the institutions in our culture—the family unit, schools, jobs, and workplaces—condition us to leave responsibility to others, to follow directions, and to do only (and only as much) as we are told.

During the average development of an individual, many influences tend *against* the formation of self-managing abilities and practices. Parents, teachers, coaches, and managers often rely on *external* reinforcement to direct behavior. They set or modify external circumstances in order to encourage people to act in certain ways. Specific behaviors are associated with certain positive or negative consequences, and, to a greater or lesser degree, the mechanisms of reinforcement persuade the child, the student, and the employee to behave in ways that are "accepted." People applying this sort of external reinforcement are often said to be "motivating" others, but the term is not strictly appropriate. Motivations are internal, individual, deeply personal impulses towards actions and behaviors. They cannot be supplied from without. When teachers "motivate" students, or managers "motivate" employees, they *infer* or *presume* the motivations that are exhibited in a person's behavior and attempt to provide external reinforcements, whether positive or negative, that will encourage or extinguish that behavior. When this succeeds, the individual has actually accepted nothing: the patterns of behavior are imposed from outside. In this process, the awareness of the need for genuinely individual, internal motivation is obscured.

In the workplace, managers commonly take advantage of this conditioning, using external reinforcement to achieve a desired outcome. "Results" earn "rewards" (and "failures" are "punished"); the better the results, the better the payoff. Managers may then attempt to manage results by promising rewards or threatening punishments (usually both). *Good* managers, however, ultimately recognize the limitations of such an approach. Managing through reinforcement is important, but it can't be confused with motivation. Successful managers learn that "performance" is the responsibility of the *performers* and that people must be motivated internally—*self-motivated*—to make the efforts required for consistent success.

The coaching system helps to *recondition* both managers and the people they manage. Old unproductive habits can be replaced by new patterns of behavior and attitudes. The practical, day-to-day procedures of the managing effort system are built on a key understanding—that "you can't *make* people work." A variety of constructive alternatives, all oriented towards developing people's internal motivation and self-management, allow managers to give up exhausting and unprofitable attempts to force employees to work. Instead, managers can begin to cultivate employees who choose, individually, to work to their current potential.

Overview: New Paradigms

The process of reconditioning begins with a review of managerial roles. As the next chapter will show, the understanding of what a manager is and does is rapidly changing. Traditional paradigms of both organizational structure and managerial functions are increasingly inappropriate to a fast-paced, global, service- and information-based economy. By considering the full spectrum of managerial roles, both conventional and innovative, it is easier to identify a manager's opportunities for coaching and to break the habit of seeing a manager as essentially a supervisor or problem-solver.

Implementing a *coaching* program, however, also requires a new approach to "results" and "performance"—the central terms of management styles based on external reinforcement.

Chapter Two distinguishes the elements of talent, effort, and opportunity in the "performance equation" that determines an individual's performance, opening up new issues and challenges for the coaching manager while also clarifying responsibilities and accountabilities. A fuller analysis of performance lays the foundation for the five major principles of the managing effort system: in Chapters Three to Seven, these principles are explained and related directly to the role of the coach. Chapters Eight to Ten set out the three basic steps in implementing your coaching system, and Chapter Eleven offers practical techniques and exercises that are useful in day-to-day coaching activities. The final chapter looks a little further ahead, suggesting how coaching may be related to a much broader "self-management culture" in which the effort grid itself is reshaped.

As any experienced manager knows, just because something is written in a book—or taught in a training course or presented from a podium—doesn't mean that it is valid. The concepts and approaches we discuss will be thought-provoking, and many of them will seem counterintuitive. However, the requisite approaches and skills are available to any thoughtful and disciplined manager. We invite you to think critically as you read this book, making decisions for yourself about what you can accept and implement in your particular environment. Good luck to you as you work with this information and the "Managing Effort" system.

IF YOU ONLY HAVE ONE WAY OF

MANAGING, YOU ONLY HAVE

ONE WAY TO SUCCEED.

Chapter One

MANAGEMENT: CONTEXT, ROLES, AND AUTHORITY

Objective

The management system described in the following chapters is a coaching system that *focuses on effort to get results*. The goal of this system, both in the long term and in day-to-day undertakings, is to create an environment that reinforces efforts and results, high achievers, and hard workers, and that extinguishes poor effort, underachievers, and low-effort workers. This goal is achieved by identifying, maintaining, and developing self-managers. This is an evolutionary process. Therefore, you can start right now, with the resources and people you already have on hand.

Over the long term, this process transfers some of the traditional functions of managers to the people they manage. But this does not mean that managers lose their influence, their authority, or their purpose. To the contrary: as employees evolve into self-managers, taking on more responsibility for their own daily activities, their long-range plans, and their careers, managers are increasingly able to pursue their most productive activities.

The difference is best understood in terms of the distinction between *direct* and *indirect* management. The direct manager is the person responsible for—and in control of—the day-to-day activities that are required to get the job done, to meet objectives, and finally to get the necessary results. And that person, it must be stressed, is the *individual employee,* not the boss, the supervisor, the "manager" so called. It is impossible to control people's behaviors and the outcomes they achieve. As a result, managers who attempt direct management use up an enormous amount of time and energy in an effort that is likely to have only limited, short-term results.

Managers cannot do their employees' jobs for them. They have their own job to do: the *indirect* management of employees, achieved by addressing time and energy to the controllable aspects of environment and infrastructure—the larger context in which employees make their efforts and achieve their results. Indirect management has little or nothing to with the immediate, detailed supervision of employees' efforts and activities, and everything to do with the conditions that affect employees' performance from day to day and month to month: selecting good people, providing the right opportunities, offering effective training, matching skills and tasks, and developing and maintaining good performers.

The Context of Management

Management is a specific form of the power relations that exist between people. In a business context, we usually view a "manager" and an "employee" as the specific players in an unequal relationship that is based on unspoken assumptions about authority, approval, and rewards. These assumptions may be explored by examining three basic models of management:

1. Command and control;
2. Fair exchange; and
3. Partnership.

These models represent a spectrum of possibilities ranging from "management," taken in its narrowest sense as the top-down direction and supervision of employees, to "leadership." The models themselves are seldom made explicit. They may not always be observed or discussed directly. They are found at the level of "ideology" and in the actions and attitudes that managers bring to their role. Understanding the most basic models of management can help us see how we may be motivated by contradictory impulses, and how these conflicts may create resistance to development or set limits on growth. We have already noted, for instance, that while we set a high value on individual responsibility, we often willingly give it up, and that as parents, teachers, or managers, we often act so as to curtail it in others. This is no simple inconsistency, but the product of tensions deep in the models we "take for granted."

Model 1: Command and Control

The command and control model is the traditional authoritarian pattern. At best, when it reflects a parent/child relationship, it is paternalistic. Followers defer to the authority of the leader, receiving security and approval in return. At worst, however, the approach is dictatorial. Leaders compel obedience. Their stock in trade is fear, intimidation, and threats of punishment. Leaders who rely on command and control play on their followers' fears: either the fear of losing desirable rewards or the open fear of unpleasant consequences. Rewards and punishments are both, of course, *results;* this model tends to focus on results, with little consideration for effort and talent.

Command and control leaders rely on organizational authority. They tend to emphasize their position, appealing to the power of their place in an organizational structure to support their commands (and to back up the "threats" that lie behind them). In business, a command and control approach typically stresses titles, levels of command, and hierarchical relations within a company. Employees who talk a lot about their job descriptions are probably part of a command and control organization: job descriptions are the place where their individual talents and efforts are related to the general mandates of the entire organization. (Significantly, too, employees often start talking about job descriptions because they are frustrated, resentful, and dissatisfied with their jobs: they may feel that their talents and efforts are not being expressed or recognized.)

A command and control approach is not always *tyrannical*. In a business environment in particular, the model offers a high degree of comfort to people who *want* structure and direction, people who prefer to let others take the burden of initiative. In extreme cases, such employees will "work to rule," relinquishing their accountability ("You told me to...") and doing just enough to create a safe environment. Things will get done, but the leader will be managing to a minimum. The hallmark of this approach is unilateral decision-making, leading to minimum creativity and growth.

In the long run, too, management by "threat" and "reward" succeeds only for as long as intimidations and incentives can be backed up. When either is revealed to be empty, command and control leaders quickly lose the respect of their followers. As a result, the command and control model can, at best, produce only short-term results. Such an approach inevitably leads to a loss of motivation, less risk-taking, and less development of employees' potential. Stated goals may be reached, but will seldom be exceeded. Where there are few opportunities for growth and progress, the best that can be expected is to maintain the status quo.

Since this approach to leadership is so limited, why is it prevalent in business, even today? Many managers will respond that it is the way to get results. In discussions on this issue, strongly results-oriented managers typically favor command and control as the means to get things "my way," "the right way," and "right away." And, granted, a command and control approach is decisive, quick, and generally clear in direction. It is also more convenient for a manager who has a well-developed strategy or game plan—it's easier just to tell people what to do than to have them propose their own projects.

Still, as we have suggested, the long-term effect of this approach is to leave all of the responsibility with the manager. If one of the main goals of leadership and management is to develop self-managing employees, the command and control model fails.

Model 2: Fair Exchange

This model appears to represent a distinct improvement on the command and control approach, as it makes the relationship between leader and follower explicit and rational. The fair exchange model does not require threats or force, and it is less likely to intimidate a follower with externally imposed consequences. Instead, it proposes an open exchange of goods or services. Generally, the time, talent, and energy of the follower is exchanged for money, security, and/or opportunity. In the best-developed forms of this approach, the terms of the arrangement are worked out in advance, and the transactions are "transparent." As well, the fair exchange approach is more than purely materialistic; it can incorporate intangible components such as job satisfaction, professional development, or personal growth.

A fair exchange approach demystifies leadership. In the business context, for example, managers claim authority not "because they are the boss" but because they have (or represent) valuable resources that can be exchanged for good performance. The hierarchical structure that characterizes a command and control organization is, to some extent, leveled out by this process of exchange. Negotiating in good faith and honoring their "contracts," managers and employees are united by the principle of fairness.

All this seems naturally fair and plausible—as it should, given its roots in market economics. However, it is still essentially *reactive* and results-driven: "You do something for me, and I will do something for you." Motivation, performance, and rewards are still considered in terms of measurable consequences, and the talents and efforts that produce the consequences scarcely enter into the calculations. As a result, the fairness of the exchange can easily be called into question. Who really deserves a bonus: a sales rep who meets a quota with a few lucky sales or a rep who works hard all month but just misses the target? No one would want to take away the lucky rep's bonus, but it seems only fair to reward effort too. *This* kind of fairness, however, is usually not part of the fair exchange model, which relies upon *incentives* such as bonuses, perks, and payoffs. To deprive the lucky performer of a bonus would, in this context, be manifestly "unfair." Every incentive, however, implies a disincentive. The hard-working underperformer may feel that he or she not only has *not* been rewarded but *has* been punished.

The fair exchange approach, unlike the command and control approach, allows a certain amount of growth. Probably the most prevalent approach used in business today, it does encourage people to improve their performance and raise productivity. But, in the long run, a fair exchange approach has to fall back on rules, regulations, and policy, or on a kind of bribery. With incentive after incentive, payoff after payoff, the system tries to keep employees motivated. It is hard, however, to keep coming up with new incentives, especially because of the escalation of expectations. There is a limit to all this, of course, and sooner or later, the cost of the incentives will cancel out the benefits of improved performance. But that limit is seldom reached, since the motivational process usually begins to backfire much sooner. Motivators can become demotivators with astonishing rapidity. Managers who are locked into a cycle of raising the stakes have made some bitter observations on human ingratitude: "We gave him a company car, and the first thing he said was 'Where's the CD player?'" Another significant problem with an approach that requires too many rules is that it also requires too much supervision, and this, in turn, can easily beget a "work-to-rule" or "union" mentality, which stifles creativity, independent action, and growth. Ask yourself if you have been in a conversation like this:

> *Manager:* Ted, can you stay late tonight? I need to have this project ready first thing tomorrow morning.
>
> *Ted:* Yes—if I can leave early on Friday to make up for it.

Despite the limitations we have sketched out, many managers see little wrong with the fair exchange model, partly because it is so natural and easy to understand. Ted's manager, above, can hardly fault him for his "quid pro quo" response. And the fair exchange model does try to treat people fairly. But it too fails to achieve the crucial goal of developing self-managers. It is a system that still requires *too much* managing.

Model 3: Partnership

This model is more of a "leadership" model than a "management" model. It goes beyond the exclusively results-oriented thinking of the command and control and fair exchange models. The leader or manager, rather than assigning tasks, imposing goals, or dictating quotas, *manages commitments* to activity and effort. In business, for example, a manager using this approach shares corporate and unit goals and spends time with the employee considering individual goals. The realization that corporate and individual goals are critical to each other sets up a positive relationship between manager and employee. Once performance objectives have been set, individuals are encouraged to develop the projects and methods that will achieve the results. The general strategy is to develop shared purposes and objectives: "That is what we want to accomplish; how can we get there?" A manager who uses this approach finds out how employees *can* accomplish shared objectives, rather than just telling them *that* they *must* or *how* they *must* do their jobs. When they participate in this process, employees know that they, not the manager or the company, own the process, are responsible for the performance, and are accountable for the results.

This leadership model also involves an exchange, but not one that is based, in a calculated way, on trading rewards for results. Instead, managers and employees make *commitments*. In return for resources and support, employees undertake various initiatives. While those initiatives are determined by performance expectations, the respect and mutual trust do not depend on results. Hard work, vigorous attempts to develop potential, and creative new approaches to goals are all given their proper value—even if the anticipated returns are not achieved. The real key to this coaching system is to recognize that people are capable of making and keeping commitments, and to encourage them to do so. The power of this concept will become clearer in our discussion of the "admission ticket" later in this book.

When results-oriented, productivity-based evaluation is complemented by possibility-directed, effort-based commitments and evaluation, performance can move beyond the limits set by a command and control or fair exchange model. In the former, performance is limited by the imagination and creativity of the leader. Few will do more than what a command and control leader wants, and most will do as little as the leader will tolerate. The fair exchange model also rewards people for doing what they are told, and so tends to prevent performance-boosting initiatives. Managers working with individual commitment, however, get team members to devise the means to reach targets, and solicit new ideas and innovative contributions. A manager who doesn't claim to know how people ought to be doing their jobs, but asks them, as the experts, how they think they might do better, unleashes their talent and imagination. As they get better and better, the manager can give them more and more room. And finally, the manager is no longer "managing people" but working with self-managers.

Managerial Roles

Most managers find this an attractive prospect, but they may express some doubt as to whether or not it is really possible: "That's all very well, but my company's not like that; the business isn't like that. *I* can't change the world!"

The world, however, is changing by itself; the principles and practices that make up the coaching program are designed to help you keep up with it. Business culture in the West has traditionally passed questions up and handed answers down. This organizational tendency, like many cultural phenomena, has become increasingly at odds with basic economic and material conditions. Even in the 1950s, many management theorists and company executives saw "top-down" bureaucratic structures as outmoded and unproductive. Subsequent events have reinforced the need to expand and transform managerial functions. National industrial economies have slowly been replaced by global information-based economies; new organizational forms have evolved, with new patterns of productivity and authority. Bureaucratic hierarchies have given way to leaner, more adaptive organizations, while labor mobility, higher levels of education and skills, the advent of the knowledge worker, and increased equality of opportunity have undermined many of the traditional foundations of top-down management. Decades of downsizing, "right-sizing," and restructuring have virtually compelled a redistribution of responsibility among executives, managers, and employees. As a result, a considerable number of managerial roles can now be identified.

Where Coaching Begins

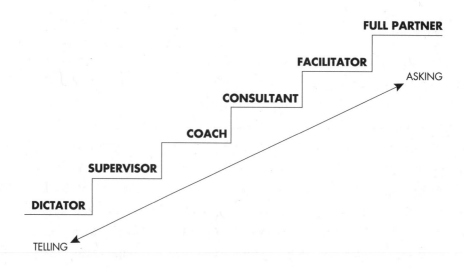

Figure 1.1
Managerial Roles

Figure 1.1 sets out the range of these roles. It is important to distinguish them clearly and to recognize their variety. Many managers tend to think of themselves as playing just one of these roles, usually one close to the bottom of the "steps."

The diversity of roles must be emphasized, if only to draw attention to the fact that a *combination* of roles is probably required to help managers respond to all the circumstances that they face. Different situations and different employees demand different management approaches.

Boss/Dictator

Every role, then, has its proper application. "Dictator" sounds bad, but in some circumstances, employees simply need to be told what to do, and all a manager must do is provide precise directions. When used deliberately, sparingly, and with a clear sense of the costs, a command and control approach can be effective.

Such "bossing," however, is a form of *direct management*. It is based on an attempt to take control of individual employees' activities and outcomes. Although old-fashioned dictators, snapping out orders, can get it right *some* of the time, the rest of the time they wear out employees, inhibit initiative, and restrict growth to what they believe to be possible or desirable. Truly dictatorial bosses do not figure in, and often do not even recognize, these costs. All the responsibility and the credit remain concentrated in them as the only authority. Relying on fear, bosses cannot *respect* the people they manage. And where respect is not offered, it is not returned.

Supervisor

The next step up, as the diagram indicates, is the role of super-visor. Managers who *monitor* employees' activities and maintain at least some distance from their routines and operations are less likely to inhibit development and growth. But this is still a form of direct management. In a closely supervised environment, employees don't feel particularly empowered, and they tend to resent the imposition of rules and regulations, and constant check-ups on their work. The supervisor is seen as an enforcer of the rules, a champion of the process and the structure, and this perception usually inhibits creativity and innovative thinking. Even the best supervisors typically reserve the final authority for themselves. Although supervised employees are allowed responsibility for their performances, the supervisor assumes responsibility for the *results*—the more or less valuable product of the employee's efforts. "Micromanagers" is the pejorative term that is used to describe "supervisor" managers. (And it is worth noting that self-managers tend not to stay very long in a "supervisor" system.)

Coaching and Beyond: The Dividing Line

A great deal of management in the past consisted of "bossing" and supervising—both essentially a means of controlling employees. Coaches, however, can be distinguished by their tendency to work "from the inside out" rather than "from the outside in." In sports, coaches drive players to reach their potential. But they also hope that individuals will *exceed* their previous performance. This sort of accomplishment can only be achieved by the individual; it cannot be done *for* a person. Personal growth is grounded in an imaginative grasp of some new possibility and in the formation of a new personal objective. It is possible to encourage a person to form such objectives, but they cannot be supplied "from the outside." Coaches, then, work to help people find their own objectives, their own enlarged sense of possibility.

Of course, coaching for improved skill is pretty much a constant for the better managers, who are always training, showing, observing, and providing feedback. But, unlike dictators and supervisors, coaches *ask* as well as *tell.* Telling— what to do, when to do it, why it must be done, how to do it, how to do it better, etc.—is an important part of any manager's job, so much so that many managers assume that it is the only part of their job. "Bossing" may seem to be the natural manage- rial function, but it puts an enormous burden on a manager who, as a human being, does not know everything, may not have the best answers, and does not have the time to oversee everyone's actions. And this burden always increases, since "bosses" unwittingly *train* their employees to wait for direction and to look to them for the answers. Let's look at the next step up.

Consultant

In the business world, consultants are often contracted to come into a company or a department to develop a strategy that will solve a problem or improve performance. A consultant is understood to be an expert in his or her field, and has the trust and approval of the client. Typically, the consultant analyzes the situation, asks a lot of questions, and then delivers a solution, gameplan, or strategy. When managers act as con- sultants, they usually approach the employee from a position of relative expertise, since they are likely to know more about the business and the situation (in fact, they may even have encountered the situation before), and can therefore guide the employee and perhaps even offer a solution or a useful strategy. However, they are careful to place the responsibility for implementation on the individual. Consultant managers may offer a lot of suggestions, but they also make it clear who owns the process. This is not a matter of "bossing"; it is a recognition of the consultant's own limitations and of the employee's strengths, abilities, opportunities, and responsibilities.

Facilitator

The next level, referred to as that of the "facilitator" in our model, represents the most important step up in the "staircase" of managerial roles. It appears, in our experience, that the most effective leaders manage with a facilitative approach—and that the approach is somewhat rare in the fast-paced corporate or sales world today. For many managers, moving to this level represents an evolution not only in style but in thinking.

Facilitators are similar to consultants. They have relevant expertise and the trust and approval of their "clients," and they begin their interaction with fact-finding and careful analysis. But there the similarity ends. As part of the questioning process, facilitators ask for the *employee's* analysis of the situation, and for his or her recommendations and proposals for dealing with issues, solving problems, or taking action. This approach opens up a new dimension of the managerial function. The act of asking shifts responsibility to the person being asked—just the place we want to encourage it. And when you ask people tough questions about their own situations, issues, or problems, you are getting them to do the hardest work there is, which is to think. The fact that thinking is such hard work probably explains why so few people regularly engage in it.

Encouraging others to make this effort is hard work itself. And it involves a distinct evolution of managerial thinking. A facilitator has the goal of getting the employee to do the hard work of thinking. To do this, he or she has to *ask*—to ask them to think about what they could be doing. This marks a shift from the natural inclination to tell people what to do. Making this transition is one of the most difficult shifts most managers must make if they see their role—and goal—as developing self-managers.

The manager may still be involved in the process of analyzing a situation and sharing the responsibility for a solution, even though this is achieved by organizing and feeding back *employees'* input. Facilitators, however, try to close the loop as quickly as possible. They get the facts out in the open, take apart a problematic situation, and then invite the *people involved* to develop the required course of action. The facilitator is on hand to guide the implementation process, but the authority and responsibility remain with those who will actually carry out new activities or apply new techniques. Their sense of ownership is a powerful motivator; as a result, facilitating managers seldom have to worry about "buy-in," since they don't have to "sell" their own proposal to the people who will carry it out.

Full Partner

Beyond consultant and facilitator lies a role we refer to as "full partner." Such a role is the logical long-term culmination of a systematic attempt to tell less and ask more, to stop pushing employees, and even, finally, to stop pulling them. Here, at the top of the staircase, is perhaps the ideal role for the manager— that of partner, not boss, who supports the development of people who can manage *themselves*. "Full partner" managers are still managers, but they are very different from conventional managers, mainly because they do not work with conventional employees. They have developed *self*-managers, who enjoy the authority and responsibility to conduct their own activities. Self-managers hardly need to be told what to do, and when they need the support of a coach, consultant, or even a facilitator, they know when and how to ask for it. The "full partner" manager, then, is primarily concerned with creating an environment that requires and reinforces excellence. Employees think, plan, work, and keep commitments to others and to themselves, while the manager coaches, consults, facilitates, and partners, as appropriate. As associates, both manager and employee work as self-managers, taking control of, and responsibility for, their proper tasks.

What Roles Do You Play?

Managers are sometimes surprised at just how many managerial roles can be distinguished, and some believe that these distinctions are purely theoretical. Many managers find themselves so preoccupied with "telling" and supervising that even those who would like to be coaches complain that, practically speaking, they just don't have the time. They know that the more they supervise, the less they coach. But there are too many emergencies, too many fires to put out, too many problems that need a quick fix. So, typically, they work out a compromise: they will supervise every day, because they have to, and they will coach, consult, and facilitate...someday, because they want to.

Most managers, when they review their options carefully, decide that a more facilitative approach would be desirable, but find that day-to-day circumstances seem to make it impossible: "I have to keep an eye on them all the time, keep them up to the mark"; "Someone's got to tell them what to do." That sort of problem-centered, results-oriented talk comes fairly naturally to managers, and it does make the idea of coaching, consulting, and facilitating seem a bit remote. And, of course, as we have noted, a certain amount of supervising, and even a certain amount of "telling" and directing, is at times appropriate.

From time to time, it may be helpful to consider your own situation. Spending all your time issuing orders or supervising activities says something not only about your people but also about the approach you take to your people. Despite your good intentions, you may be "pushing," telling people what to do in too much detail, and reinforcing their dependency on you. You can't be blamed for resenting the demands they make on you, but you can't really blame them for making them! When you are caught up in day-to-day supervising, you just don't have the time for the kind of asking and listening that helps would-be self-managers work out their growth plans.

Day-to-Day Coaching

Every day offers plenty of opportunities for bossing and supervising—for direct management. But it is essential to extend your efforts and activities in *indirect* management. That is why we propose a coaching system that is made up of simple, practical steps that you can take *every day* to help develop a environment in which consistent effort, strong talents, effective performance, and good results will be properly assessed and appreciated. As a daily practice, coaching can be just as straight-forward and intuitive as issuing orders or overseeing activities— it's simply a matter of identifying who is responsible for what, and making sure those responsibilities are clear to everyone involved. As a manager, it is not really your responsibility to get the daily sales, the weekly production output, or the monthly reports. That is the responsibility of the individual salespeople, the workers on the shop floor, or the staff analysts. *They* must make the effort and get those results. *Your* responsibility is to see that the best possible people are on the job, that they know what they have to do, and that they have the resources they need to do it. That is why you are accountable for the results. When both you and your people recognize your proper responsibilities, many more opportunities for coaching—and consulting, facilitating, and partnering—will arise naturally. In part, that will be because your managerial time and effort will be devoted to those with the greater potential: your golden eagles and effort eagles.

Developing Self-Managers

Managers who make the breakthrough to coaching (and beyond) no longer do a number of things that make up the daily activities of many results-focused managers. However, the new roles do not involve any less energy and time. Coaches are not only distinguished by what they do not do. A manager who tries to shift from telling to asking takes on a very difficult challenge: encouraging people to set objectives, make commitments, and follow through. Traditional "dictators" and supervisors are not troubled by this challenge. They do it all themselves—or try to. When they succeed (in the short term), their approach rewards simple obedience, creates a burdensome dependency, and can drive potential self-managers away.

Managers who take the crucial step to the coaching role want to create independence and initiative. A hockey coach, for instance, can *order* a player to score, but when the player does so, it is the *player's* accomplishment: he wasn't just being obedient. And the coach can't jump onto the ice and do it himself (no matter how much he wants to). Coaches, consultants, and facilitators must all work to break old dependencies and to foster self-assurance and autonomy. As you think about your own managerial role, and realize that the overriding objective is to support independent thinking and self-management, you will become more aware of the behaviors and actions that help you achieve this goal, as well as those that work against you. Here are two questions we suggest managers ask themselves before and during any interaction with an employee:

- Is what I am doing, or about to do, creating or continuing a dependency, or is it creating independence and independent thinking?
- Am I providing the occasion and the resources to let others take responsibility for that which belongs to them?

Resistance to Coaching

Managers who want to move up the "staircase," evolving their approach to leading others, can expect resistance from some of their employees. First, and more importantly, however, they may have to overcome some *internal* resistance, an unconscious bias towards telling rather than asking, and reinforcing rather than motivating, that is deeply rooted in our business culture. Most people will agree in principle that managers would be well advised not to restrict themselves to "dictator" and "supervisor" roles. But many managers find it difficult to put the theory into practice. They express a number of anxieties and foresee a variety of potential problems.

Getting Out of Step

One common concern has to do with the way managers themselves are managed or supervised. Managers who are not coached or consulted themselves may feel unwilling, or even afraid, to take a different approach with their own teams. They may feel that asking, rather than telling, will set them at odds with the company or corporate culture, that such an approach won't be sanctioned "upstairs." However, if you are a manager who isn't being coached or consulted but is just being told to hit certain targets or reach imposed objectives, it's possible that no one is looking too hard at how you do it. When a company is not interested in your input and only interested in your output, there is considerable room left for your own initiative and creativity. The stronger the concern with results, the stronger the emphasis on "getting the job done," no matter how. And if you are getting the results in ways that increase your satisfaction and reduce your stress, while improving overall performance, upper management is not likely to complain!

Control

Managers may also resist the move from telling to asking because it seems to involve a loss of control. But what does it mean to be "in control"? If you spend a lot of time giving orders and keeping tabs on the consequences, it is easy to tell yourself that you are in control of things. (In fact, you may just be *reacting* to things, barely *controlling* them at all.) Managers who monitor their own performance in these terms sometimes fear that they will lose credibility if they stop issuing directives and start asking questions: "What will my guys think if I start wringing my hands and saying 'What are we going to do?'" The quick answer is "Don't wring your hands, and *ask better questions!*" When you challenge your employees with direct, specific questions on goals, commitments, and activities ("What do you need to do to reach these objectives?" or "How do you plan to meet your targets this month?"), no one will think you have lost your sense of purpose and direction. Rather, they will see you as a leader.

Successful coaching is a matter of taking control and giving control. That is, managers must take control of their controllables—the thinking, the attitude, the behavior, and the approach that they take, and the external conditions of the work and the workplace that they really can determine. This is the proper area of indirect management. At the same time, managers must recognize that, to a greater or lesser degree, there are always *uncontrollable* factors that shape and determine every outcome. A failure to distinguish between controllables and uncontrollables encourages a manager to act as a direct manager and to try to take responsibility for every circumstance, every result, and everybody. Self-managers, whether managers or employees, manage their effort and activities—the things they can control—to get results; they keep the focus on circumstances and influences that can be directly affected. The enlightened coach realizes, and acts on, the fact that you cannot command and control other people's success.

Authority

Perhaps the most complex issue that arises when you shift from telling to asking has to do with *authority.* Won't such a change in approach appear to diminish the manager's authority? And won't this undermine the orderly functioning of a team, a department, or a division?

1. Organizational Authority

A manager's authority may derive simply from his or her position in a company. Although this is a purely formal authority (the manager *borrows* the power to direct and reward from the larger, more powerful organization), it must not be underestimated. In every institution, a wealth of implications attaches to merely being in a certain place and having a certain title. Teachers experience this all the time. Even on the first day of a new class, just walking *behind* the desk grants them a whole range of privileges and establishes them in a position of power over every other person in the room.

Organizational authority, however, is conferred, not earned, and it can easily be lost. People recognize the authority of a designated leader because they are familiar with the codes and customs of an institution. But, because of this familiarity, they are quick to perceive ways in which a person does not conform to institutional demands and expectations. Only a few deviations will persuade others that the delegated authority has been misplaced and that the wrong person has been put in charge.

2. Experiential Authority

More persuasive sources of authority are education, experience, and personal accomplishments, which are the products of self-investment and personal growth. People are more likely to acknowledge a manager's experiential authority, since it is obviously related to individual attributes, rather than to organizational dictates. A manager's right to direct activities and reward results is usually more acceptable when it is based on his or her familiarity with the employee's job, the company's larger projects, or the industry.

However, this very familiarity can bring the manager too close to the day-to-day operations that ought to be left to employees. At best, experienced managers may interfere with employees' activities in an attempt to share (or impose) their abilities and understanding. At worst, they may demonstrate a "know-it-all" attitude that enforces a set routine and restricts employees' initiative. Any person's experience, after all, is necessarily limited, and his or her experiential authority is similarly limited. Qualifications in one specific area may not carry much weight in another. Consider the recently graduated MBA who is assigned to reorganize a service department: spreadsheets and project-planning software, no matter how useful, may fail to impress an installer with thirty years of experience in the field. In such cases, managers often fall back on organizational authority, using it to push through their plans. And, as a rule, the more they push, the more they get shoved back.

3. Personal Authority

When experiential authority is not enough, there is an alternative to simply insisting on one's position. Perhaps the most compelling and lasting authority is based on personal power, on the talent and effort that you display by taking control of controllables, making commitments, and following through. Managers are used to looking for talent and effort in their employees, but sometimes they don't realize that employees look for the same attributes in them. Managers may also mistake the sort of talents that will earn them respect. Managers who become too involved in their employees' jobs may be *trying* to demonstrate their good qualities, but the attempt can easily misfire. Managers are most valued when they show themselves to be good *managers.* Salespeople, for example, will appreciate someone who is good at managing a sales staff and a sales office—but they may resent someone who tries to get too involved in their successful sales process.

Authority and Responsibility

If the most secure foundation of authority is, as we have suggested, an exemplary personal power, then a manager's authority and responsibility coincide in *self-management.* The best managers are the best *self*-managers; they provide a compelling example of the skills and effort patterns that get results, and they know, from experience, how those skills and efforts are nurtured. As a result, they can coach, consult, and facilitate their people's self-management potential, making the most of the strengths and abilities their employees offer. Employees are often willing to grant authority and offer loyalty to a self-managing manager who is skillful at facilitating their growth and development as self-managers.

Self-Managers

This coaching system is designed, finally, to encourage employees to become better self-managers, to take control of their effort (their most important controllable), and to actively seek out coaching for growth and development. Such employees will allow you to manage in new and creative ways. Working with self-managers gives you more time, more independence, and less stress. Self-managers don't need an manager to tell them what to do or a supervisor hovering at their side. They may need a coach, sometimes a consultant, and perhaps a facilitator to help them set goals and expectations, review successes, and make bigger and better commitments. And when their self-management skills are highly developed, they will soon find that the manager has become more of a partner in their business than a boss.

Where Can I Find Them?

Self-management potential can be *developed.* Research and testing show that self-management potential is linked to the capacity for effort (a "will-do" attribute). This capacity appears to be inherent. Nevertheless, people have varying levels of self-management potential, and so will learn and adapt in a self-management environment at different rates. High or low effort levels, if well established over a long period of time, tend to remain stable. They can change, but are less likely to vary than medium levels of effort, which can be affected by results and reinforcements.

There are two ways to get self-managers (or high-potential self-managers) on your team. One way is to *recruit* them. This may require some adjustments of your selection process. Many recruiting and hiring practices are not well-adapted to attract or detect either self-management potential or good effort history. And it's worth mentioning that most self-managers are already employed—of course! If you are recruiting among people who are out of work and not actively developing themselves, you aren't likely to spot many. But self-managers *can* be attracted, not only by a job and its compensation but by the career prospects a position offers. Self-managers may be "disturbable" rather than "disturbed." They want to get somewhere, rather than get *away* from their current situation. Since self-managers usually have clear long-range objectives, they can be interested in opportunities that will help them get there.

Not every manager, however, has the flexibility to go off and start hiring an entire staff of self-managers. Fortunately, there is a second way to get self-managers on your team: *recognizing the ones that you already have.* For, as we have mentioned, many managers do not spare the time to think about the people who are doing well, working hard, and satisfying expectations; they are too busy worrying about, and coaxing, their problem cases. When you stop telling and start listening, you will begin to hear more from your self-managers. If you can stop simply paying off good results and start recognizing the value of good effort, they will have even more to say. Finally, if you can stop trying to manage by results and start managing by effort and commitment, you'll see the good team that was there all along, and you'll see it getting better.

PERFORMANCE =

TALENT x EFFORT x OPPORTUNITY

Chapter Two

THE PERFORMANCE EQUATION

Results: The Number-One Priority

You wouldn't be reading this book if you weren't interested in improving the results of your company, division, or team. Results have the power of an accomplished fact. They are the incontrovertible evidence of "success" and "failure." Often, the best stories managers have to tell turn on unforeseen results— last-minute saves and against-the-odds, surprise victories. An emphasis on the unexpected success tends to discount or even ignore the performance that preceded it.

Performance, Results, and Success

Results are, inescapably, the final measure of performance, whether we are speaking of individuals, companies, or whole markets. Performance is the means to results; it is what people do and how they perform that produce the results. But performance cannot simply be equated with results.

You know you are expected to get results—it's not likely you see it as an option. You are accountable for your results. You accept this without argument. Yet what you are held accountable for is not fully within your control. We are all familiar with the many uncontrollable factors that influence our results, particularly when we must achieve results through others—our staff or team of employees. The list of uncontrollables is long, including (to mention only a few)

- the price of raw materials
- your market

- the economy
- the competitive environment
- government regulation
- your operating budget

These uncontrollables can have a considerable impact on results we achieve, but they need not have any direct influence on our performance. Good performance is based on devoting effort to what can be controlled, and refusing to waste energy in attempts to direct unpredictable circumstances.

As a consequence, there is also an important distinction to be made between results and *success.* We are accustomed to associate the two very closely and to judge people's success according to the results they achieve and the rewards they display. That quick, external judgment, however, can be quite inaccurate. Success is, of course, associated with good results, but it is determined by good performance—that's what leads to good results. The most successful people are not necessarily those who make the most sales, earn the highest salaries, or receive the most external reinforcement. Genuine success also requires that they consciously realize their best potential. That success can only be accurately identified and fully enjoyed by the individual who takes control of the controllables and takes responsibility for effort. It does not depend on externals, and it can even survive when results are not all that could be desired.

The Performance Equation

Being held accountable for results is a fact of management life. That accountability won't go away. How then, given all the things out of your control, can you manage? This is where the distinction between performance and results gets interesting—and crucially useful to effective managers. One of the most critical factors in getting results is *how your people perform.* As long as performance and results are not clearly distinguished, it's easy to think that performance is just another of the uncontrollables: you've got good performers, and you've got underperformers, and sometimes, unfortunately, you have poor performers.

The "performance equation" breaks performance down into its main elements and groups them as shown below. When we examine these elements, we can see how they interact to produce results.

PERFORMANCE =

TALENT   X   **EFFORT**   X   **OPPORTUNITY**

INHERENT   TRAINABLE   **QUALITY**   **QUANTITY**   FIT TO JOB   FIT TO
ATTITUDE   BEHAVIOR   CULTURE

Figure 2.1
The Performance Equation

It is possible to make rough calculations as to how talent, effort, and opportunity will work together to determine performance. The calculated value of the three factors is produced by multiplication, not by addition. Each factor, then, makes its own distinctive contribution; high levels of ability, for example, can offset a lower attitude rating, and while well-qualified people may survive in any opportunity, they will excel only in a well-matched opportunity. Deficiencies in any category don't just lower the final value of performance: they are likely to reduce the value sharply. And if there is a zero score in any category, the calculated value must also be zero, no matter how high the other values may be.

When we distinguish these three components, it becomes possible, first, to *analyze* performance issues, so as to influence performance and maximize results. This is an important first step in coaching. Hockey coaches, for example, are certainly concerned about the final score of each game, but their real work is focused on the players' ongoing performance, from shift to shift and from game to game. Once performance issues have been examined in detail, it is then possible to determine the necessary coaching. Talent, effort, and environment issues cannot all be treated in the same way—and it must be recognized that some of these issues are simply beyond a manager's control. The performance equation helps show where managers can *productively* direct their efforts, energy, and intelligence—that is, to areas where the most impact and growth are possible.

The Talent Factor

Kinds of Talent

Matching employees to productive opportunities is often a matter of recognizing their talents. Managers agree that "ability" or "talent" is a defining attribute of their best performers. The terms refer to a variety of competencies. Good performance is generally associated with special skills, knowledge, capabilities, relevant experience, and education. The best performers are also said to possess less easily documented abilities: "street smarts," "empathy," or "know-how."

Employees bring their talent to the job with them. As a result, it might seem that managers have little control over this performance factor. This is certainly true in the case of managers who restrict themselves to "bossing" and "supervising." You can't *tell* someone to act more skillfully or to show more know-how. (Actually, you can, and some managers do. The problem, of course, is that telling people to smarten up doesn't make them any smarter.) Coaches, however, can have a considerable influence over the performance of their people. Because they concentrate on identifying potential and encouraging its development, they can deal with talent issues, and coaching strategies can be devised to target specific individuals and situations.

Talent Issues

It is important, first, to distinguish two kinds of talent that contribute to performance: inherent and trainable. "Inherent talent," which tends to remain constant, includes such things as intelligence, personality, empathy, and common sense—all the fairly intangible qualities that we sum up when we speak of a person's "current potential." (The distinction between *current* and *ultimate* potential will be explored in more detail in later chapters. Here, it is sufficient to note that any assessment of employees' potential indicates not so much what they are capable of doing as where they are capable of *starting*. A person's ultimate potential is not easily or directly evaluated.) The components of inherent talent are evident to most observers, even though they may not be easily documented or tested. They become obvious after long acquaintance, since they are part of an individual's makeup. Inherent talent is a crucial consideration during selection and assessment. It is essential to attract and select people with high potential, since it can't be developed on the job, and it is a waste of time and money to train people who have little or no potential.

"Trainable talent," in contrast, is not given but *learned,* and it can be tested. It includes such things as product knowledge, acquaintance with procedures and routines, familiarity with the job functions, and various kinds of job skills. The skills that make up trainable talent are developed through experience acquired on the job and through formal education and training. Thus a person's level of trainable talent can be increased, given the appropriate learning experiences or training. Because this kind of talent is easily documented (by academic standings, resumés, and licenses or certificates) it often counts heavily in selection and hiring processes, sometimes to the exclusion of inherent talent, which is only reflected indirectly in a person's recorded work history.

Talent: Whose Responsibility?

The distinction between inherent and trainable talents helps clarify *responsibilities* for talent issues. Generally, the development of talent is a shared responsibility. A person brings to the job the required inherent talents and at least some of the necessary trainable talents. A manager must assist in developing the trainable talents to suit the immediate, specific demands of the position. Some talent issues, however, are beyond the scope of the manager. Deficiencies in *inherent* talent, in particular, cannot be compensated for by training. Intelligence, empathy, and common sense can hardly be taught. Nor can they be developed by reproofs or exhortations.

When selection and hiring processes are well-conducted, inherent talent issues seldom arise. If they do, it is important to save your energy and attention for things that you *can* influence. Remember the performance equation: a person's inherent talent sets one of the factors at a constant value. But you can still try to achieve higher performance by influencing the *trainable* factor. From the coach's perspective, this is the key issue. The coach's role is to provide the necessary training— the "can-do" aspect of the job—and ongoing consultation concerning skills, knowledge, and strategies.

Together, inherent and trainable talent account for the "can-do" factor in performance. Barring a lucky accident, there's no success without sufficient talent. Every sports coach knows that, and talent is usually the first thing that is scouted in new players. In business organizations and in sports, teams need people with good skills and good potential.

Attitude and Effort Issues

The "Will-Do" Component

Good *performance*, however, depends on more than just raw talent and knowledge of the game. Top performers don't just *have* abilities; they *use* them. Managers also refer to a number of good *habits* that are typical of good employees: they are "hard-working," "determined," "disciplined," "motivated," "persistent," and "committed." All of these terms reflect the importance of *effort* in achieving results. The right attitude and consistent effort are crucial.

A person's habitual attitude and effort make up the "will-do" component of the performance equation. This "will-do" component, like inherent talent, usually doesn't vary. People's attitudes (their habits of thought) and efforts (habits of behavior) tend to be pretty much formed by the time managers encounter them. It's often claimed that "past performance predicts future performance." Much more accurate, however, are the observations that "past attitude predicts future attitude" and that "past effort predicts future effort." Attitude and effort tend to remain consistent; habits are, after all, very difficult to change. People who work hard tend to continue to work hard. We often say they have a "work ethic."

Attitude is often associated with the *quality* of results, and effort with their *quantity.* We have all known people who work hard but have a poor attitude towards their work. They may get a lot done, but perhaps not much that will last or that will lead to new growth. Alternatively, people may have a very good attitude but not make a great effort. They don't get very much done, but what does get done is perceived as both valuable and satisfying. Managers may support this combination, misled by the "country club" atmosphere it creates. Positive feelings, plenty of job satisfaction, good intentions, and high morale all make for a very attractive work environment. This may offset any shortfall in the quantity of results—if only in the short term. Some managers then compound the issue by reacting to the shortfall, announcing a "strategic revolution" that will turn today's "country club" into tomorrow's "efficient, results-driven organization." A better approach, of course, is to balance quality and quantity, attitude and effort, by ensuring that the environment provides good performers with empathetic approval.

Attitude, Effort, and Responsibility

The question of how the talent and environmental aspects of a person's performance are shared between the person and the coach is a common topic of discussion and even argument. The debate is invariably prolonged by the question, "Who is responsible for employees' effort, their "will-do," their attitude?" The ensuing discussions, often lively and even passionate, always illuminate the special nature of *managerial* responsibility in the middle element of the performance equation.

How would you respond? Your answer is likely related directly to the approach you normally take in dealing with an employee's "will-do."

If you are like many managers, you may feel that it is important for you to take an active role in making people work hard. This is a very common view, and it is supported by compelling arguments. First, managers feel responsible for, and know they are accountable for, departmental or team results. This sense of accountability can be a major pressure, and it can produce a great deal of stress. To compensate, many managers feel impelled to push for more efforts, to tell people to do things, to exhort employees to get on with the job. This reaction is consistent with the well-established notion that a manager's job is to *pass down directions* to employees and to motivate them to improve their attitudes and work harder.

Second, many managers are naturally supportive and caring people, who feel responsible not only for results but also for their people. Most managers genuinely want to see their employees succeed, and when they can see that a performance problem is an effort issue, they are inclined to get involved, to help out, and to provide the impetus they see is lacking.

The position you take on this "will-do" question and the way you behave as a result may actually be the major determinant of your success and longevity as a manager. The question "Who is responsible for employees' effort?" is simple, but the stakes are high. And the answer to the question?

Attitude and effort belong 100% to the individual!

That's right: as a manager, you are *not responsible* for your employees' attitude and effort, but you are 100% responsible for your own attitude and effort. Each individual is responsible for his or her own attitude and effort.

The Opportunity Factor

The Importance of "Fit"
This element of performance involves "fit"—both to the job and to the larger culture in which the work is done. The importance

of fit is well known. Many success stories depend on having someone in the right place at the right time. Sometimes the success occurs no matter who the person may be. *Consistent* good performance, however, depends on having the *right* person in the *right* job and in the *right* environment. This is a matter of the individual's fit to the opportunity or role, which is determined by a variety of components.

The benefits of matching an employee's abilities, background, and goals to the opportunity are evident. One of a manager's chief priorities is to put talented people, with the right background and right experience, into the right positions. Making sure that the initial "fit" is a good one saves money and time, and improves performance for the individual and the manager.

The opportunity factor relates to the specific tasks and functions of the job or role. The essential questions are, what is the job, and does the person fit? Giving the right person the right opportunity is a critical performance factor.

Responsibility

Who is responsible for making sure of the fit to the job? Effective managers realize that this has to be a shared responsibility. When placing an employee in a new position, the manager and the employee are both responsible for exchanging information candidly and truthfully. The manager must communicate the specific nature of the opportunity clearly, and the candidate must express his or her relative fitness honestly. This exchange, in which both parties try to determine the suitability of the candidate for the job, is central to taking what we call a career-planning approach.

The Cultural Factor

The arrow that leads from opportunity to culture reflects a shift of attention away from opportunity factors such as territory or marketplace, existing clients, products and services, or pay systems and towards the immediate environment in which day-to-day work takes place. Corporate structures, products, procedures, and markets, among other things, create the context in which certain actions are required, expected, or simply considered "normal." When an individual shares (or accepts) these norms, there is a good fit to culture. This can be seen at work in professional sports, when players are traded. Hard-working, talented players often perform better in the new surroundings, not because they are working any harder or have developed new skills, but because they have the coaching, team support, and chances to play that make the most of their strengths. The opposite can also happen: it's easy enough to think of very high-level executives, for instance, who turn one company around but fail to work the same magic when they are recruited to save another one.

The most important cultural factor is the manager. A good match between the employee and the manager is essential, not so much for performance (that is determined by fit to job) as for *retention.*

By definition, everyone in a given environment shares the responsibility for that environment. Recognizing this is often an important step forward for new managers, who may not be aware that they share this responsibility with others. Indeed, the company and the manager have a major share, but every person is an important part of the whole. Intelligent managers work to create environments that support high-effort, performance-oriented employees, but they also seek input from employees to develop shared expectations as to how managers and employees will work together and how the work will be accomplished.

Focusing on Effort

As the preceding discussion of the performance equation has shown, the factors that determine performance—and get results—are more or less controllable by the individual and by the manager. The special emphases of the managing effort system described in this book stem from the critical point that attitude and effort are fully and solely the responsibility of the individual. This point, however, can create a dilemma for many well-meaning managers. For usually, when employees fail to perform well after their initial training and development, it is because of a "will-do" issue, an issue involving attitude and effort. Occasionally a poor fit with the opportunity or environment is to blame, and sometimes a talent issue can be identified, but most managers will acknowledge (and thousands have told us!) that poor or inconsistent effort is at the root of most performance problems. So what can a manager do about poor performance? If effort and attitude are solely the responsibility of the employee, what can a manager do to get people to work hard, or harder, or more consistently?

The approach that rookie managers and coaches take (and even some veterans) is to get involved in the employee's "will-do" issue. And when they do so, they typically begin by *coaxing*.

Coaxing

Coaxing is a very common response to what most managers perceive as the challenge of an employee's poor performance. Because managers enjoy a challenge and because they are commonly conditioned to deal with problems rather than growth, they tend to devote themselves to low-effort employees. Behind this approach is the assumption that good performers, and even average performers, will get on with the job without being *made* to; the manager chooses to concentrate on the people who won't do the job "unless I make them." Finally, however, managers have few options but to plead for more effort. They fail to distinguish between motivation and reinforcement, and attempt to "motivate" individuals by manipulating external reinforcements. What was intended to be coaching becomes *coaxing*.

There are two principal coaxing strategies: "attitude management" and "behavior modification." Both share, however, a focus on doing things *to* people. Exercises in attitude management (pump-up sessions, incentive programs, pep talks, motivational seminars) are some of the coaxing manager's main tools. It's worth noting that such exercises may produce good effects almost immediately, at least in the short term, partly because they involve a sharp discontinuity with work and the workplace and partly because of the positive reinforcement. No wonder people feel better about their work problems when they attend a "personal power" seminar or a morale-building retreat—they aren't at work! With the full approval of their managers, they have been allowed to set aside the day-to-day reality of their performance problems. Even better, they have been promised that someone else, a motivational guru, will solve their problems. The results are usually reminiscent of old-time revival meetings. Plenty of people get "saved," but most of them backslide as soon as the preacher leaves town. Attitude management, since it usually attempts only to alter attitudes, without cultivating any associated behavioral changes, has little long-term effect. The "honeymoon glow" soon fades. The new attitude is eroded, often within days or even hours, because the habitual attitude of the individual reasserts itself or because the same old behaviors eventually erode the new attitude.

Another common approach is to change behavior by introducing new procedures, carrying out new activities, setting new reporting systems in action, distributing new planning tools, and so on. The focus, once again, is on externals. Changes are made not in the person but in the workplace. There is the same "holiday" effect of getting away from the old workplace, but it can't last long. Changing *routines* can bring about apparent changes in behavior, but they do not go very deep. As often as coaxing managers shuffle the deck, they will still find themselves playing with the same old cards. Everyone likes a change, but behavioral changes without deeper attitudinal reforms are also ineffective in the long run.

"Coaxing" approaches have low long-term success rates because, although they are meant to work from the outside in, they usually deal exclusively in externals. When employees are coaxed, they seldom *internalize* the manager's priorities or values. Coaxing approaches also tend to address *either* attitude *or* effort. More effective coaching, however, deals with both attitude *and* effort, and works from the inside out.

Handling Effort Issues

Simply distinguishing effort issues from talent issues eliminates one of the most common and least productive strategies managers use to deal with poor performance: taking a "can-do" approach to a "will-do" problem. Effort issues simply cannot be resolved by skill training. Effort issues have little to do with a lack of talent, yet time and time again managers will take people who aren't working very hard and retrain them, send them on courses, or even work with them to show them once again how the job is done. Managers almost instinctively assume that poor performance is a skills problem, especially managers who have become managers in part because of their own success in developing their skills and competencies. As a result, they may see no alternative solution.

Good attitudes and high levels of effort constitute the "will-do" element in performance. When lack of effort is an issue, managers are dealing with a "will-do" issue, one that is, strictly speaking, beyond their control. Working hard and having a good work ethic are commitments that start *within* the individual. It is a simple fact that *you can't make people work.* You may demand, and receive, compliance, but you cannot command *commitment.* As a result, it's managers who believe they can make their employees work who end up working the hardest of all. They command people to work, beg them to work, tempt them to work; they describe the rewards people will receive if they work or threaten them with the painful consequences of not working; they invite people to work, urge them to work, and talk about the benefits of work. Managers who occupy themselves in this way are usually the busiest people in the organization, often exhibiting admirably high levels of effort. But this managerial performance is not always associated with the desired long-term employee performance, and it is difficult to keep up. It takes a lot of effort to make people work, and that effort is almost always misplaced, as it is used up in trying to take hold of uncontrollables. The returns are generally so disproportionately small that burn-out is inevitable.

As we have emphasized, effort and attitude must be recognized as the responsibility of the individual, not of the manager. Managers are sometimes troubled by this concept, perhaps because it goes against the grain of a common understanding of managerial functions. As we have noted, when managers are asked, "Who is responsible for your people's attitudes?" many of them answer, "I am, I guess. Well, it's up to me to keep them motivated...." But when we ask managers, "Never mind your staff. Who's responsible for *your* attitude?" managers never transfer the responsibility to *their* bosses or superiors: "I am, of course; my attitude is my own responsibility."

If managers hold themselves responsible for their own attitudes, why do they treat their employees differently? In fact, there are a number of reasons that managers are perhaps too willing to assume the burden of their employees' responsibilities. In a traditional business culture, responsibility and accountability tend to be passed upward through the various levels of command. This tendency is effective for the purposes of planning and communication. However, when authority and initiative are always to be found at a higher level, it seems natural for attitude and motivation to be the concern of the manager, not the employee.

The Effort Grid

The distinction between "can-do" and "will-do" issues is critical, and many managers, not having a system that allows them to make such a distinction, misplace their valuable time and energy. The effort grid, already mentioned briefly in the Preface, is an analytic tool that was developed for use in selection, development, and retention. Based on the essential distinction between talent and effort, the grid organizes the various challenges managers face when dealing with job applicants and with new and long-term employees. In the selection and coaching process, the effort grid serves as a decision matrix, identifying the most and least attractive candidates, and sorting out coaching needs and options according to varying degrees of talent and effort. It helps determine probable returns on investment (ROI)—investments of training time and budgets, coaching efforts, and career development. By helping managers make rational, well-founded choices, the effort grid minimizes the probability of serious performance and retention problems, and maximizes the returns on the coaching and training energy expended by managers.

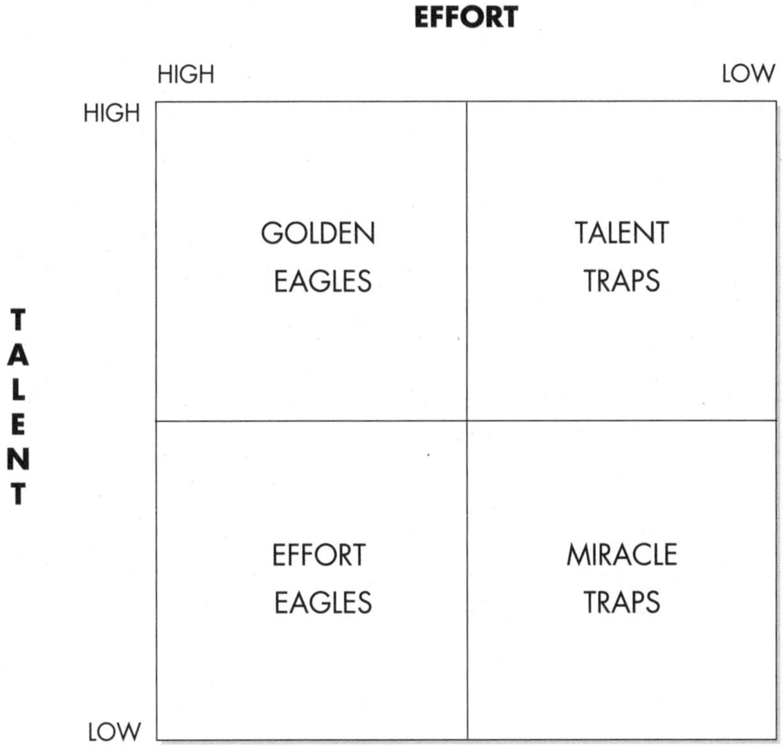

EFFORT

	HIGH	LOW
HIGH	GOLDEN EAGLES	TALENT TRAPS
LOW	EFFORT EAGLES	MIRACLE TRAPS

(Left axis labeled vertically: **TALENT**)

Figure 2.2
The Effort Grid

In day-to-day management, the effort grid can also help you choose appropriate coaching strategies, by distinguishing four categories, or quadrants, that can be used to assess employee performance:

- golden eagles (high talent and high effort)
- effort eagles (low talent but high effort)
- talent traps (high talent but low effort)
- miracle traps (low talent and low effort)

The grid is, of course, based on the performance equation. Only two success factors are emphasized; while opportunity is a key determinant of performance, it is not really an attribute of the individual performer. In dealing with employees in any of these categories, *modifications* of opportunity are often a manager's first response.

Coaching the Effort Grid

Coaxing managers, as we noted, use their powers of persuasion (or intimidation) to get desired activities, efforts, or results. They typically run up against the fact that people can't be made to work; they fail to distinguish complex "will-do" problems from simple "can-do" issues. Coaches, by contrast, *begin* by separating talent and effort issues and allocating the responsibility for these issues appropriately. Then, rather than simply attempting to stipulate new limits for performance, they help individuals set their own objectives for improvement and development.

The utility of the effort grid is easily demonstrated. Try this simple exercise:

1. List your employees.
2. Estimate the amount of time you devote to each one—both directly and indirectly.
3. Assign each employee to an ability/effort quadrant.

Compare the results of Steps 2 and 3. Which quadrants are getting most of your time? Many managers find that a typical distribution looks like Figure 2.3. Usually, most of the time goes to the talent traps, in an effort to get more effort, and to the miracle traps, in an effort to create a miracle in the absence of sufficient talent and effort. Much less time goes to the top-performing golden eagles and to the hard-working effort eagles.

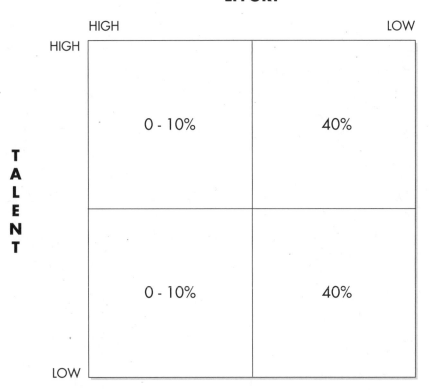

EFFORT

Figure 2.3
The Coaxing Grid

Look at your grid again and consider how you are directing your time and energy. Are you putting most of your resources into the quadrants that are getting the results you need? Are you spending time with hard workers and high achievers? If so, you are using your own managerial effort effectively and productively. And you probably have no risk of burn-out, since your effort is getting good returns.

With an equal number of employees in each box, the ideal analysis would look like this:

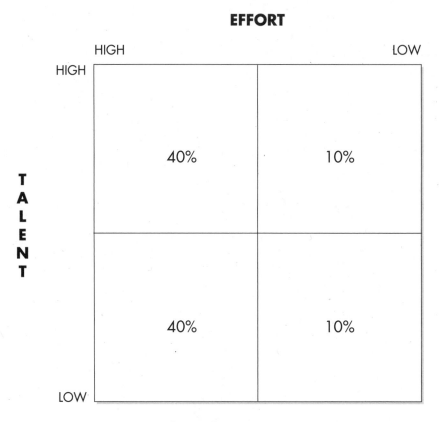

EFFORT

Figure 2.4
The Coaching Grid

To improve performance and maximize results, the best managers spend as much as 80% of their time on their effort performers and the people with the most trainable potential. Talent traps and miracle traps get only as much support as they need to help them decide to *change* or to leave.

Golden Eagles

One of the main purposes of the managing effort system is to ensure that your investments of managerial energy and resources *increase* in proportion to your employees' effort levels. Typically, the most rewarding employees are experienced ones who have supplemented good inherent talents with on-the-job training and who demonstrate consistently high levels of effort. They can be fun and challenging to work with; they are also easy to talk to, since they offer three things to discuss and to reinforce: talent, effort, and the good results they are getting. Most managers tell us that working with golden eagles is not really work at all—and that time spent with them passes quickly and enjoyably.

If you are used to devoting most of your attention to poor performers and problem cases, you may have to make some readjustments. Golden eagles don't need to be encouraged to work hard, and they don't expect *you* to tell them what to do. Observing their strong performance and good results, some managers may feel inclined to step back: "If it ain't broke, don't fix it." This attitude, however, reflects an orientation towards results (and "problems"). Even where there are no problems, there are still plenty of opportunities.

While they enjoy congratulations and rewards, golden eagles also need to be challenged. They know they're doing well, but do they know why? Golden eagles may be unconsciously competent. A manager's responsibility is to help golden eagles reinforce, expand, and maintain their conscious competence. They often have good ideas about how they can do better. Golden eagles will respond well, then, if you ask them what you can do to help them build on their achievements. The best approach is to ask, first, "What do you do well?" The easiest and quickest way to improve, after all, is simply to do what you do well more often and consistently. A second question is perhaps even more important: "What do you see as your areas for growth and development?" Allow golden eagles to propose and develop their own growth objectives. Training must only be offered when it is asked for. Even better, have them train others. Making presentations at meetings and mentoring effort eagles are often considered effective reinforcements for golden eagles.

Effort Eagles

Effort eagles (employees with high levels of effort but low talent levels) also deserve a considerable investment of your time and attention. Here, the general approach is to reinforce the effort and develop the skills. Typically, effort eagles require experience and training. New hires, for example, or employees whose experience has become outdated because of industry or technical changes have plenty of potential for good perform- ance, if they can sustain high levels of effort. The first step is to reinforce good efforts. The second step is to identify any talent issues that can be addressed by training. If inherent talents are the issue, there is little a manager can do, apart from reinforcing and increasing effort activities, and seeking possible adjustments to the opportunity. Even where training and coaching will help overcome a talent shortcoming, however, managers must ensure that effort eagles *take* the opportunity for development, rather than having it forced upon them. Managers must take the same approach as with golden eagles, taking care, however, to reinforce both the positive aspect of the effort eagles' performance and the need for their development. Allow them to formulate their own needs. In this way, effort eagles will make commitments and will not simply assume that you are going to make things better for them. Effort behaviors must be regularly recognized and reinforced. Effort eagles have plenty of

potential, but if they learn that poor performance, for whatever reason, is acceptable, they might never develop into
golden eagles.

Talent Traps

Most managers are very familiar with talent traps. Many spend a
lot of their time with them. Talent traps, it may be noted, aren't
necessarily doing anything "bad." They have learned exactly how
much (or, unfortunately, how little) they have to do to get by.
They do just that much, and they often seem to be the least
stressed people on the team. They've got the time to enjoy the
atmosphere, after all. Devotees of the status quo, talent traps
are easily capable of compliance. But their *commitment* is
seldom offered.

Employees who have the talent but just lack effort know how
to awaken a manager's coaxing instincts. Managers typically
have high energy levels: it's as though they can't really *believe*
that a talented person won't make an effort. For many managers,
a talent trap is an irresistible challenge. And the talent traps
know it: "I just don't seem to be able to get this going";
"Can't figure out what's wrong. I just don't seem to be able to
get it together...." In other words, "Motivate me, or take over!"
Few managers can refuse.

But they *must* refuse. Although it may be hard to break habits,
the best approach to take with talent traps leads *away* from
them. Even if you ignore talent traps and take away all the time
you formerly devoted to them, their productivity usually
remains about the same. They continue to do just about what
they want to do, and they continue to hit the minimum targets
that keep them employed. The worst that can happen, then, is
more of the same old thing. If talent traps produce better-than-
usual results but continue to show little effort, no special

treatment is required—unless you choose to point out, directly and explicitly, that it is only the results that keep talent traps in their positions. More importantly, if they occasionally exhibit a particularly good effort, a skillful manager will take the opportunity to reinforce it.

When you restrict yourself to reinforcing the talent traps' results, you will find that you have plenty of time and resources freed up for your better performers. The redirection of attention will probably be noticed, and some talent traps will get the picture. When they see that you are no longer coaxing, no longer prepared to take the initiative for their activity, and that you are now paying attention to employees who make an effort, they may be motivated to get the attention they are used to. If the only way to do that is to make an effort, a few talent traps may be turned around. Make it clear that your coaxing days are over, and send a clear message: "I'm not going to save you any more." If they begin to show increased effort levels, be quick with positive responses and reinforcement. Let them know that you appreciate their efforts, and when it seems appropriate, offer support. Be careful, however, not to fall into the old role again. The questions to address to talent traps who want to change are coaching questions:

- How can *you* improve?
- What are you going to do?

Avoid coaxing:

- Let's work through this together.
- Let's spend some time on this.
- Come on, you can do it. Just get going!

Miracle Traps

Almost every manager has a story (either an incredible one,

when a miracle occurred, or a sad one, when nothing happened) about these employees. Whether they slip through the selection and hiring process or run into difficulties on the job, they pose a problem. Effort eagles challenge a manager's coaching skills, and even talent traps can respond to the right sort of approach. A combination of low talent and low effort, however, is practically impossible to address effectively. Trying to make good an employee's shortcomings in talent and effort is one of the most punishing and unproductive tasks a manager can undertake, yet it is also a common one. Whether from a sense of responsibility or from feelings of sympathy, managers often protect these weak performers, hanging on in the hope that a miracle will occur and justify their faith.

Miracle traps receive this support because they are often likeable and sympathetic. Miracle traps are often the legacy of managers who trusted their instincts and hired on the basis of "fit," to the exclusion of talent and effort. They hold their positions because, at some point, a hiring manager mistook "someone who can get along with us" for "someone who can work well for us."

Effective coaching, however, is not about liking or disliking. Managers must spend the least time with this group of employees, not to "reject" or "exclude" them, but to make it clear, both to the miracle traps and to the other groups, where they intend to supply reinforcement and support. It's only fair to face the facts and explain the situation to these poor performers. In the absence of trainable potential and the attitudes needed to make training work, there is little the manager can offer. You can, given sufficient time and resources, make anyone successful, but is it worth the price? Attention is more profitably directed elsewhere. And, finally, so are most miracle traps. By focusing on top performers, on well-meaning effort eagles, and on turnaround talent traps, you have the potential to improve your department's performers and performance. Miracle traps ultimately hurt themselves and others.

Miracle traps are often revealed to be a consequence of *opportunity* issues, a simple case of the wrong person in the wrong place. This may have to do with the original selection process, or it may be the result of organizational evolution or change. In some cases, otherwise well-qualified employees *become* incompetent, a sort of reverse "Peter Principle." Acting directly to eliminate misplaced employees may seem severe. Still, redirection or termination may, in the long run, be a kindness.

Return on Energy

The effort grid is not meant to discriminate between "good" and "bad" employees; rather, it groups employees according to a variety of effective management strategies. All of these strategies are designed to maximize your "return on effort," a kind of long-term "return" on the investment of time, energy, and creativity that you make, as a manager, in each individual on your team. Golden eagles, obviously, promise the highest returns on energy, both in the short and long term. They require the least direct intervention; the manager consults, facilitates, expedites their initiatives, and enjoys the achievements they bring about. Effort eagles, by contrast, may provide only an average, and even a poor, short-term return. In the long term, however, they promise very good returns on effort. If you have the resources and the time to train effort eagles and they sustain their good effort behavior, they can become golden eagles.

Talent traps may, surprisingly, offer *high* short-term returns. That is part of the "trap": they are willingly led and quickly agree to your proposals for development, improvement, retraining, motivational workshops, attitude management, incentive packages, and any other devices to boost their effort levels. No one is more grateful for a fresh start or a second chance. And they will continue to be grateful and receptive long after a manager has exhausted himself or herself inventing new motivational schemes. In the long run, talent traps provide a very poor return on effort.

Mapping the effort grid against results helps clarify the kinds of rational choices a manager must make.

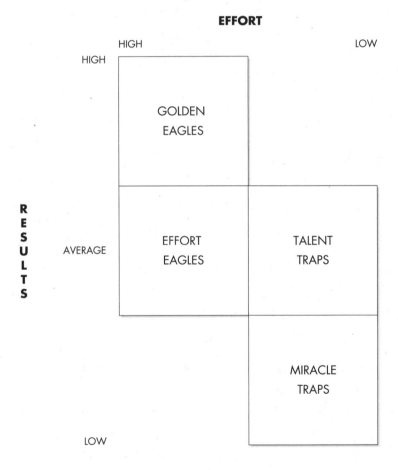

EFFORT

Figure 2.5
The Results Grid

Judging both by results (the final priority) and ROI (a manager's daily priority), a manager needs to concentrate managerial effort on golden eagles and effort eagles, while monitoring talent traps and miracle traps. An analogy with financial investing illustrates these priorities. It's only natural to *invest more* where there is *more potential* to get something back. Many management processes, however, direct the largest allocation to the least promising investments. When they have the time to think about their financial investments, managers don't look for red-hot markets that might collapse at any moment or for poorly performing funds in no-hope sectors. They ought to use the same good sense in their day-to-day operations. Misplaced investments of time and energy in talent traps and miracle traps will provide, at the very best, a short-term success, a kind of maintenance management. And look at what is being maintained: the *poorest* performers, the "won't-dos." Meanwhile, the can-dos and the will-dos are left to get on with it, with reduced coaching. This neglect does not go unnoticed.

The solution? Stop coaxing "won't-dos" and concentrate on coaching the "will-dos." A simple effort grid analysis allows you to direct your managerial resources to situations that will produce results, rather than exhaust your energy and bankrupt your morale. Should you *avoid* effort issues? Of course not. But you must not support, coax, or reinforce people for non-effort, especially when it means ignoring the people who are working hard and showing good potential for improvement. It is neither possible nor practical to try to reform the "won't-dos" by doing something *to* them or *for* them; they must make the changes themselves.

How can you help them achieve attitudinal *and* behavioral changes that will reinforce each other? That is the largest topic of this book. But the first step is clear. You must start by recognizing and identifying the issues *precisely,* so as to avoid irrelevant responses. Then, you can begin managing and coaching effort to get results by systematically applying five essential coaching principles:

- expectations dictate performance
- reinforce positive behaviors and attitudes
- motivation comes from within
- maximize return on energy
- manage by effort

In some management models, the five principles listed above are recognized *after* the fact, as lessons of experience, explanations of why things turned out the way they did. Results-driven management, when it allows for any reflection, is typically retrospective. The lessons learned are seldom applied towards prospective events, and when they are, they are rarely *applied* systematically and consistently. Events get in the way, demanding a reaction.

In the next chapter, we will begin by addressing the first principle: *expectations dictate performance.* A second, related principle—*reinforce positive behaviors and attitudes*—will be discussed in the following chapter. In both chapters, we will stress the *internal* dimension of these processes. A proper recognition of this dimension is crucial to effective coaching. In Chapter Five, the central principle of *motivation* will be explored; this discussion will be supplemented, in Chapters Six and Seven, by an analysis of the themes of *maximizing returns on energy* and *managing effort.*

GOOD COACHING SETS POSITIVE EXPECTATIONS, NOT LIMITATIONS.

Chapter Three

EXPECTATIONS DICTATE PERFORMANCE

Setting Expectations — The Self-Fulfilling Prophecy

Expectations dictate performance. This principle of the self-fulfilling prophecy is, perhaps, the most powerful principle of psychology and the most powerful tool for the coach. In every context and in every activity, whatever people expect of themselves almost always occurs. People sometimes fail to appreciate the power of this principle because of the common confusion between performance and results, and the associated equation of results and success. It is not true, of course, that we always get the results that we need, want, or wish for. Every *result* has an uncontrollable dimension. Performance, however, like genuine success, lies largely within our control.

If you think you can, or think you can't, you're right.

We almost always get the *performance* that we expect, which can be good or bad, depending on the quality and the level of our expectations. Knowing this, a coach works to help people set, and then reset, expectations, so as to continually raise the level of performance.

The coach's role is to participate actively in the process of setting expectations. Sometimes people are not aware of this process or of the fact that it is an *ongoing* process. Expectations are determined by a wide range of factors. Many expectations are formed at an early stage of individual development, by personal experience and circumstances, and they are strongly reinforced by family, friends, peers, and society. We tend to take such expectations for granted, and we do not really expect them to change dramatically. In fact, "maturity" is often understood in terms of "knowing one's limits," that is, discriminating between reasonable and unreasonable expectations, and accepting certain limitations accordingly.

Such expectations, however, even though they seem so "natural," set only an *artificial* limit to possibilities. There is nothing irrevocable in the way expectations determine and restrict potential performance. For years, it was an accepted *fact* that the mile could not be run in less than four minutes. Since 1954, however, when Roger Bannister broke the four-minute barrier, increasingly shorter times have been recorded, primarily due to a change in *expectations;* the length of a mile and a minute remain unchanged.

Restrictive expectations take many forms. Stereotypes, industry standards, sales ratios, and labeling, for instance, not only condition us to expect certain kinds of behavior but also blind us to all the behavior that refutes these notions. Reputation has a similar effect: once a person, a group, or an organization acquires a reputation, whether it is good or bad, people will be strongly inclined to see only what confirms their expectations and to discount everything else. Even a *good* reputation, however, can restrict an individual's potential, especially in organizational environments. A person who becomes well-known as a problem-solver, for instance, may get all the problem projects and may not have a chance to try innovative or independent assignments. The coach's role, as a result, usually involves working *against* labels, stereotypes, and reputations—or at least against the idea that they set limits to performance.

Resetting Expectations

Expectations can restrict performance, but they can also release potential, when we recognize that they are *made*, not given, and that we may *create* expectations for others and ourselves.

Externally imposing quotas or defining specific standards for behavior and activity can backfire by setting the standard or expectation too low. External quotas and standards typically stem from an attempt to control results. And in practice, they can *set limits* to activity: they indicate just how far people have to go, or how much they have to do, before they can *stop*. Although managers usually intend quotas or company averages to be criteria for success, they can actually serve as criteria for failure, for they represent the least that can be done. As a result, the quota or minimum standard serves most directly to indicate an acceptable, but not necessarily desirable, level of perform-ance or activity. Operating in this way leads to "so-so" or "same old, same old" results, since nothing changes. (A popular definition of insanity is to keep on doing the same things but expect different results.)

Good intentions and well-meaning directives from a sales manager can actually create the wrong expectation. Consider the following example. A sales manager with a large Canadian insurance company (we'll call him Dave) was describing a challenging selection process that he used to test candidates' potential for success in life insurance sales. A key step was to have the candidate complete seventy-five "market surveys," approaching seventy-five people to discover their opinions on life insurance: what they thought of it, why they bought it, whether they would ever purchase more, etc. The survey form also asked for referrals—that is, the names of other people the candidate could survey.

Dave imposed a two-week time limit on this exercise. That meant, he explained, that the candidates would have to do their surveys in the evening and on weekends, since most of them were already fully employed. The exercise was deliberately intended as a hurdle: the candidate had to make a commitment and complete the assignment in order to move forward in the selection and hiring process. At the same time, he could point out to the candidates that doing these surveys was very similar to the prospecting work they would have to do to build a life insurance practice.

Those who passed the "hurdle" learned about Dave's criterion for success in life insurance sales, which he explained as the "10-3-1 rule." It takes ten contacts to get three appointments, and three appointments to get one sale. For insurance people, this is a well-established industry average. The problem is that no one person is necessarily average, especially new agents. Nevertheless, Dave would then tell his candidates that achieving one hundred sales in the first year would be a good start in the business, and a fairly reliable indication of potential for long-term success.

When Dave had finished describing his process, we wrote "10-3-1" on a flipchart; underneath that, we wrote "__-__-2": "2" for two sales a week, or one hundred sales a year. Then we asked Dave to fill in the blanks—to explain how the industry rule applied in that weekly schedule. That was easy: "20-6-2." Then his face fell, as he realized that he had been setting the expected number of sales calls at just *twenty a week*—less than four calls a day. In reality, it is unlikely that a new agent would be able to develop and sustain a successful business at that level of activity. And he was presenting these restrictive expectations to people who had been required, just to have a chance at the job, to complete seventy-five market surveys, on evenings and weekends, over a two-week period. Dave was saying, in effect, "Now that you have passed the hurdle and become a full-time agent, you don't have to work as hard."

The "10-3-1" rule, like any industry standard, represents a broad generalization that is not strictly applicable to any individual. Using it to set expectations is likely to restrict performance rather than encourage effort. On the basis of our analysis, it was clear that a better way to set initial expectations would be to involve the new agents in the process, asking something like this:

"Based on your experiences with the market surveys, how many prospects do you think you could contact if you were working at it full-time?"

Then, over the first few weeks, the responsible new agents (who have committed themselves to being hard-working and self-starting) could be allowed to find their own levels of maximum activity.

From a coaching perspective, setting expectations is an open-ended, *dynamic* process that is continually suggesting possibilities, rather than setting limits to effort. In this process, expectations are continually established, fulfilled, and then *reset.* The constant renewal of this process is crucial, as it helps to shift the focus away from the past (what *has* been done) and towards the future (all that can be done). The satisfaction of meeting an externally imposed quota, after all, has to do mainly with being finished and looking back at what has been completed. The satisfaction of fulfilling expectations, however, is more closely related to a sense of *achievement* and the impetus to *begin* again. Past accomplishments are most valuable when they are used to create specific possibilities for the future. For instance, if a salesperson has achieved an "eleven calls, two appointments, one sale (11-2-1)" ratio, there are several ways to improve performance. The obvious goal is to get more sales (11-2-2, for instance), but working on calling and or selling skills to achieve a 9-3-1 ratio also constitutes improved performance. As these examples suggest, the strong connection between expectations and performance extends into *results;* it is also deeply grounded in another factor we have considered.

Figure 3.1
Foundations of Results

Conscious competence—knowing clearly what you do well and how you do it—is the most basic source of personal power that, finally, drives results. Good managers encourage their people to expand and maintain this self-knowledge. By identifying competence, reinforcing it to encourage self-confidence, and constantly increasing the level of expectations, coaching managers can promote a continuous growth in productivity, a growth that is increasingly self-sustaining. At that point, the coach's belief is an "add-on." It's nice to have, but it is not central to the process of setting expectations and achieving goals. A good example of this came from Jack Kemp, former Buffalo Bills quarterback and long-time political figure in the United States. Speaking at a conference in New Orleans some years ago, Kemp recalled his first year of college football. His coach had taken him aside early in the season and told him he believed Jack was the one player on the team who had a legitimate chance of making it as a pro. He concluded by saying, "Don't tell anyone we had this discussion!"

Jack had already been "busting his tail," as he put it, and he already believed he had the potential, but with the added expectation from his coach, he started working even harder. Four years later, Jack and three others from that first-year team were drafted by pro teams. And, said Jack, "Guess what the coach had said to all four of us that first season?" In fact, Jack suspected that the coach had probably had the same discussion with quite a few of the players. But Jack and the three others actually succeeded because they had already *expected* to succeed. The external belief expressed by the coach corresponded to, and strengthened, their own internal expectation. The coach's encouragement, by itself, couldn't do the job: players who didn't *begin* with the expectation didn't really have a chance.

It is worth stressing, once again, that coaching expectations is not a matter of demanding certain results and then "turning up the pressure." Expectations are set and reset in a reciprocal, negotiated process between the coach and the individual, a process that is based on dissonance theory. Effective managers help performers establish expectations for their *performance*. Of course, these expectations are influenced by the results that must be achieved, but they are also determined by the individual's potential. As a result, both the coach and the individual must have an accurate perception of this potential, so as to set expectations that are challenging and worthwhile, yet attainable with effort.

The difference between expectations and actual performance —the "incentive gap," according to dissonance theory—can be a powerful motivator. People naturally want to "close the gap," so long as its width is carefully calculated. That is, if expectations are set too high, they may seem unreachable: people are likely to feel that the best they can do is "tie or lose."

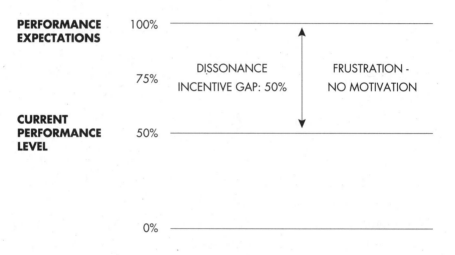

Figure 3.2
Dissonance Theory: Unrealistic Gap

Unrealistically high expectations are likely to produce frustration, and in the long run are demotivating. At the same time, if the difference seems too small, people may see no value in the achievement or may not be aware of the need to stretch. Performance will stop at the expected point; motivation decreases directly as the incentive gap decreases.

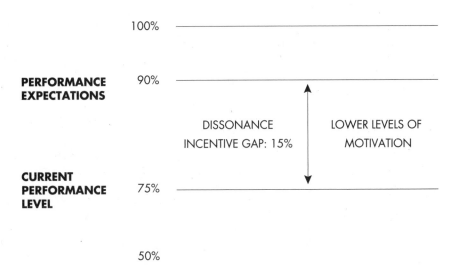

Figure 3.3
Dissonance Theory: Demotivating Gap

Whether expectations are set too high or too low, complacency can be the result. Faced with an unreasonable expectation, people will say, "I couldn't do that, even if I *were* any better (so why try to improve?)." Low expectations lead people to say, "That was easy. I don't need to worry about anything."

An ideal incentive gap as shown in Figure 3.4—a roughly 25% gap between past performance and current expectation—represents a challenge that can be met. Effective managers and coaches create the conditions for worthwhile activity, by helping set or reinforce expectations that are challenging, yet attainable through a committed effort.

Self-Managers

Although easy in theory, determining the "incentive gap" that is appropriate for an employee may be difficult in practice. As we have already noted, you must begin with an accurate appraisal of the person's potential, an appraisal that is more or less in

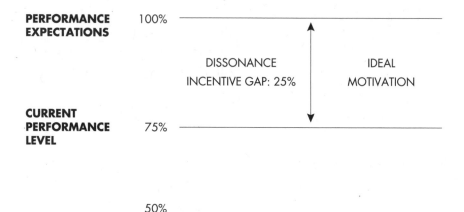

PERFORMANCE
EXPECTATIONS 100%

DISSONANCE
INCENTIVE GAP: 25%

IDEAL
MOTIVATION

CURRENT
PERFORMANCE 75%
LEVEL

50%

Figure 3.4
Dissonance Theory: Ideal Gap

agreement with the individual's self-evaluations. Careful observation of previous performance and effort can help, along with psychological tools that help measure "achievement potential." People with high achievement potential usually set their expectations high—often significantly higher than others would. In general, private expectations are as much as 25% higher than public expectations: high-achievement individuals may expect even more of themselves. It is also worth noting that only *current* potential (a person's scope for effort and achievement as it currently stands, given the existing circumstances of opportunity, effort history, and talent) can be measured with any accuracy. A person's *absolute* potential—the scope he or she can attain through experience, self-development, and self-confidence—is never finally reached. It is like the horizon, which constantly recedes as we advance.

There is no purely objective way to make the appraisals needed to set an incentive gap. How can you tell, then, whether you are suggesting expectations that are too high or too low? The answer is obvious: ask the person, or, better yet, let the employee tell you what to expect. After all, your employees know, much better than you do, how much talent they have and how much effort they are willing to expend. If you have a job to get done, it just makes sense, in allocating your resources, to find out how people can contribute to the objective, rather than telling them what they must do. More importantly, when you stop telling and start asking, you encourage the development of self-managers, who pursue their *personal best,* rather than any company average.

As illustrated in Figure 3.1, the power of expectation has its sources in conscious competence and self-confidence. Expectations, all by themselves, don't produce the desired performance, but they do directly influence the effort. A well-calculated incentive gap will cause the individual to do the work, to make the additional effort, to persist in trying —because "I know I can do it." On the other hand, the expectation that it will be too tough or just impossible will lead to reduced effort, discouragement, and even quitting in the face of the obstacle or challenge. The opening chapter of Norman Vincent Peale's seminal book, *The Power of Positive Thinking,* has as its title "Believe in Yourself." Is belief in oneself not the most powerful of all expectations?

The challenge for a thinking manager or coach lies in getting individual performers to develop beliefs and set expectations that will cause them to make a real effort. One way to do this is to *stop* setting expectations for your people and begin to improve your ability to ask them what *their* expectations are. This is a very powerful approach for establishing daily or weekly efforts or work activities. And when you ask them what their expectations are, what their work ethic is, what they are prepared to do—essentially, "How hard can you work?"—you are showing trust and respect for them as individuals; this will help you move towards meaningful decisions about what a person will do. It is always fair, and advisable, to ask individuals to set their own expectations for results—and then hold them accountable. When people are asked questions about their expectations for controllables (effort), they can usually answer, even if they have little knowledge or experience in the business, because they manage and control their own effort. If the expectation has to do with controllables, it can be turned into a commitment, for which the individual may be held responsible.

BEHAVIORS AND ATTITUDES

ARE STRENGTHENED BY

POSITIVE CONSEQUENCES.

Chapter Four

REINFORCE POSITIVE BEHAVIORS AND ATTITUDES

Reinforcement Theory

Consider the basic premises of reinforcement theory:

1. Behaviors and attitudes that are *positively* reinforced will be repeated.
2. Behaviors and attitudes that are not *positively* reinforced will disappear over time.
3. Behaviors and attitudes that are *negatively* reinforced will not be repeated.

Positive reinforcement is essential to conditioning, socialization, and learning. When we are rewarded for the behaviors or attitudes that parents, teachers, and employers desire, we tend to repeat them, in the hopes of continued rewards. In time, the desired behavior becomes habitual, although it continues to require the support of reinforcement. Even the most well-established habits of thought or action will tend to be extinguished eventually if they are not reinforced.

Reinforcement and Learning

Negative reinforcement is also an important part of our development, since socialization also requires the suppression of undesirable behavior. Sometimes, unfortunately, the two modes of reinforcement are confused, and negative reinforcement is mistaken for a means to encourage desired behavior. The command "Don't do that!" says nothing about what *needs to* be done, but this obvious fact is often overlooked in practice. Negative reinforcement can be a relatively effective way to extinguish behavior, but it creates no specific expectations for future desired behavior. As a result, it has a limited role in an effective coaching program: ideally, as much as 90% of a coach's time and energy is spent on positively reinforcing desirable attitudes and behavior, and as little as 10% on extinguishing unwanted behavior.

LEARNING MODEL	DESCRIPTION	LEARNING POTENTIAL	LABEL
I. Conscious Competence	Learning from what we do well	FULL	Self-Confident
Conscious Incompetence	Learning from what we don't do well		
II. Unconscious Incompetence Conscious Competence	Learning only from what we do well	1/2	Arrogant
III. Unconscious Competence Conscious Incompetence	Learning only from what we don't do well	1/2	Self-Doubting
IV. Unconscious	No learning		

Figure 4.1
Learning Models

We do, of course, learn from our mistakes, especially if we are punished for them. Negative reinforcement has a place—it's what we often refer to as the school of hard knocks. But the most we learn, when we are lucky, is not to make the same mistakes again. Negative reinforcement develops "conscious incompetence," an awareness of what we do *not* do well. We learn *more,* and, psychologists tell us, we learn *better,* from our successes. When our actions or attitudes are positively reinforced, we develop "conscious competence," an awareness of what we do well. We learn what we are expected to do in the future, and we have an incentive (the expectation of reward). Basically, the positive reinforcement keeps us doing the same thing and encourages us to do it more often.

The fullest learning potential involves both conscious competence and conscious incompetence: knowing what we do well and knowing what we must improve. Accordingly, good coaches focus on developing both areas. They use reinforcement to respond both to the *quantity* of the effort and the *quality* of the effort that determine performance and get results. In this way, coaches help people become aware of their attitudes and their potential for effort, which are not always accurately reflected by the objective results. The point of the process is to recognize what has *been* accomplished and, at the same time, set expectations for *future* performance, looking ahead to what *can* and *will* be done.

Reinforcement and Motivation

Conventionally, managers are accustomed to providing both positive and negative reinforcement. However, external reinforcement is often surprisingly ineffective as a long-term motivator. As we have already noted, most managers will finally admit that "you can't *make* people work."

There are a number of reasons. In some management environments, for instance, reinforcement tends to be primarily *negative*—a punishment for failure, rather than a reward for results. As noted earlier, negative reinforcement can be very effective in extinguishing certain kinds of behavior and attitudes, but it does nothing to encourage more productive or successful efforts. And even when they are positive, the customary reinforcements tend to have only a short-term effect.

Last month's performance bonus, for instance, is not likely to affect this month's efforts. External positive reinforcement must always be renewed, if the desired behavior is to be sustained. Managers may find it difficult simply to keep the reinforcement coming, and that will only maintain the status quo. An organization driven by positive external reinforcements will only be able to achieve growth by constantly "upping the ante," and promising more and better rewards for more and better results.

All of these disadvantages stem from two interacting issues: a failure to distinguish between performance and results, and a confusion between external reinforcements (rewards and punishments that *follow* results) and internal motivations (individual choices and commitments that *precede* performance). Typically, reinforcement, positive or negative, is geared entirely towards outcomes, rather than performance and potential. As a result, good behavior, attitudes, and efforts are reinforced only "by proxy" and only when the results are good too. Unfortunately, if the results are good, even poor attitudes or low levels of effort may be indirectly supported. Sometimes even the best effort doesn't succeed; at other times, success is achieved without effort, through simple good luck, timing, or coincidence. When only the results are used to evaluate performance and to allocate reinforcements, the genuine potential of an employee can be overlooked.

Self-Managers + Self-Reinforcement = Motivation

A coaching manager, then, reinforces both the efforts and attitudes that determine performance and the results that are achieved, and for 90% of the time, the reinforcement is *positive*. The most effective manager devotes his or her own time and energy to those who demonstrate good performance and results. These are strong, positive reinforcements; after all, your time and energy are valuable to you, so they are valuable to your employees as well. The response also encourages and sustains employees' own *self*-reinforcement. People usually know when they have made a good effort or achieved good results, and that awareness can be a powerful source of satisfaction and renewed initiative. All the more so, then, when the awareness is echoed, even augmented, by the indirect manager. In the long run, it is strong, positive self-reinforcement that enables an individual to persist.

Meaningful positive reinforcement, then, is used to sustain good performance and results. In an ideal situation, external reinforcements "match" internal motivations; indirect management (from the outside) and direct management (from the inside) intersect in good performance, good results, and success. There are two ways in which this match can be made. The first, less reliable, way is to provide the right kinds of reinforcements and to keep on doing so. Employers, teachers, and parents try to provide rewards for behaviors and attitudes, rewards that are appropriate both in kind and in quantity. But there is no way to be certain that the individual will see these rewards as commensurable with his or her personal sense of achievement. The second, more straightforward, way is to *internalize* the external reinforcement, to make it part of one's own self-reinforcing strategy. In either case, it is important to note that the match is always a matter of individual perception.

But what about poor performance and results? Certainly, they must not be *rewarded.* And they must only be *punished* in a minority of cases, where there are specific attitudes or behaviors that must be extinguished. In the majority of cases, however, punishments will not encourage employees to improve their efforts or help them discover new ways to approach assignments. The most appropriate and effective strategy, then, is simply to *withhold* positive reinforcement. When done systematically, this is a form of negative reinforcement that does not involve any direct or external response. It is simply a steady refusal to react to, support, correct, or interfere with undesired behaviors and inadequate achievement. Coaches systematically reinforce and support good effort, good attitudes, good performance, and good results. Just as systematically, they refuse to reinforce a poor effort or wrong behavior.

Refusing to reinforce poor performance or results helps to break people's conventional reliance on *external* reinforcements. We are accustomed to thinking of reward and punishment as things administered by others; our early experiences and learning teach us to regard other people—parents, peers, teachers, and employers—as the source of approval and acceptance. But internal reinforcements, such as a sense of accomplishment, a conviction of rightness, or the feeling of success, are the genuine sources of long-term reinforcement and motivation. The structures of our society, education, and work, however, can obscure the importance of internal reinforcements. There are always plenty of people ready to tell us what to do and reinforce our behavior accordingly. And there are many managers and parents who will take on the full-time role of directing others by trying to manage reinforcements. As a result, the people who are managed come to believe that they need constant external reinforcement and that *any* kind of attention, even if it is negative reinforcement, is better than no attention at all. This kind of "over-management" prevents the development of self-managers and may detract from the development of self-reinforcing behavior and understanding on the part of the individual.

The ultimate value of reinforcement is its role in supporting and corroborating the individual's internal sense of achievement and satisfaction. (A cash bonus, a typical external reinforcement, has no necessary correlation with such internal motivations; it is meant as a kind of "payoff," but there may very well be no relationship between the external and internal.) Coaches and self-managers make a distinction between internal motivations and external reinforcements: the first are provided by the individual self-manager, the *direct* manager, and the second, by the coach, the *indirect* manager. As a result, self-managers do not depend solely on results and approval from others for their reinforcement; they can feel they are doing well even without external approval, even when the desired results are not yet apparent.

Managers commonly supply external reinforcements predicated on results. The effective coach, however, offers qualitative reinforcement as well as quantitative reinforcement. The latter corresponds directly and measurably to the results achieved, but the former confirms, indirectly and qualitatively, the investment of time, energy, and effort. Through qualitative reinforcements, the coach checks on an individual's internal reinforcement and coaches the self-reinforcement process itself. In this way, the coach can influence motivations as well as behaviors. By helping to determine the conditions in which people will perform well and enjoy the internal self-reinforcements that follow good performance, and by allowing self-managers to set their own expectations, coaches let people create and enjoy the conditions of their own success.

COACHES MUST REINFORCE,

BUT CAN'T MOTIVATE.

Chapter Five

MOTIVATION COMES FROM WITHIN

Expectations, Reinforcement, and Motivation

The third basic principle—that motivation comes from within—is strongly connected to the first and second principles. Expectations and motivations are related. We expect others to act in accordance with what we assume to be their inner motives, and we interpret their behavior in terms of these motivations. We know from experience that any expectations we set for *ourselves* are driven by our own personal motivations.

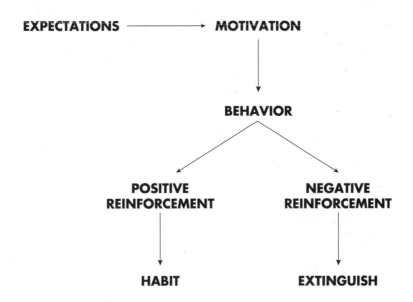

Figure 5.1
From Motivation to Habit

Reinforcements and motivations are also related. External reinforcement, whether positive or negative, is a response to behavior, and so, indirectly, a response to the motivations that produce behavior. As we have noted, however, the critical distinction between reinforcement and motivation is often overlooked in practice. Motivation logically precedes behavior, and, unlike behavior, it remains essentially internal. At best, we can guess what motivates a person's action or behavior, but we can never know for sure. (This is why coaches *ask* rather than *tell:* the more they listen, the better their guesses about players' motivations.)

Any behavior that is not the simple product of rigid external conditioning is a direct expression of internal motivations. External reinforcements follow behavior as a direct response, but only to the behavior, not necessarily to the original motivation. As we have noted, positive external reinforcement encourages the repetition of behavior and the formation of habits; negative external reinforcements extinguish behavior, but provide no specific direction for future activity. Both kinds of reinforcement, however, can have no *direct* effect on the motivation from which behavior proceeds, unless the external and internal "match." External reinforcements can modify motivation only slowly and indirectly, if at all.

You Can't Motivate Somebody Else

The common confusion between reinforcement and motivation often leads us to think and to say that we are "motivating" people when in fact we are only reinforcing their behavior. At best, in fact, we are able to make good inferences about a person's private motivation; then we devise reinforcements that are appropriate to the kind of *behavior* that such a motivation would produce. Sometimes this is easy. It's safe for an employer to assume, for example, that employees are motivated by a desire for financial security, and the appropriate reinforcements are easy to choose. It is more difficult, however, to decide what reinforcements will elicit better-than-average performance, extra effort, or improved results. Most people do a job in order to make money. But people who do a *great* job have other motivations—more personal and more internal—that drive them, that keep their effort levels high.

Since managers are well aware of the importance of having people who are highly motivated to work, take on tasks, and produce good results, they devote a lot of time and attention to this issue. Working with managers in the last two decades, we have often asked, "What are your key responsibilities as a person who must manage, coach, and lead others?" The most common answer (often the first answer) is "Motivating others." Not surprisingly, "motivating others" also heads the list when we ask managers to name the most challenging aspects of their management, coaching, or leadership roles.

Motivation is central to effective management, but managers often look for it in the wrong places. Many "motivational" schemes fall short because they attempt to *supply* motivations "from the outside" and because they make incorrect assumptions about people's individual motivations. As a result, these schemes offer *irrelevant* reinforcements. (The promise of a cruise has no positive effect on a sales rep who hates being on boats; promotion to supervisor at the home office has no attraction to someone who likes the freedom of being out on the road.) They also fail because, typically, what they offer are *external* reinforcements. Even when a manager correctly identifies a person's genuine motivation, well-calculated reinforcements provide direct support for the specific behavior that flows from the motivation, and only for a short time. External rewards (a bonus, a cruise, or a lunch with the president) can encourage a desired behavior but typically have no long-lasting effect. Reinforcing ongoing behavior relies upon a constant renewal of rewards and punishments, and every parent and manager will tell you how exhausting that can be.

"Push" and "Pull"

People's behavior can very generally be described in one of two ways: either they are "pushed" or they are "pulled." At a very basic level, people either act so as to avoid unpleasant objects or consequences or to approach desirable circumstances and situations. Although these are very different kinds of movement, the difference cannot always be observed in actual behavior: the same actions may derive from a "push" or a "pull". For instance, one employee may work hard to meet a Friday deadline so as to win approval, enjoy achieving an objective, and have a free weekend. Another may work hard just to finish on time, escape a supervisor's displeasure, and avoid having to take work home on the weekend. To an observer, the behaviors are the same, but the underlying responses to consequences are different.

External "Push" and "Pull"

The "push" and "pull" dynamic is an essential part of both external reinforcement and internal motivation. If you are a manager who believes you are responsible for motivating others, you have little choice but to resort to *external* "pushing" or "pulling"—either creating conditions or consequences that people will want to avoid, or setting out attractive consequences that they will want to approach. Managerial "pushing" plays on people's fears of punishment, loss, or failure. "Pulling" appeals to their desires for a win or a reward. Both approaches, however, can have only a limited effect. From the very outset, you are attempting to use external means to achieve an internal result. Managers who "push" typically try to impose standards, put poor performers "on probation," or threaten underachievers with loss of privilege, income, or even employment.

If you have ever attempted "push" motivation, you have probably discovered that it *sometimes* works: a "problem" employee may make the effort needed to achieve the level of performance that will prevent the threatened punishment. You may also have noticed, however (and this is borne out by our own research), that the renewed effort lasts only about as long as it takes to remove the threat. Once the employee finds a "comfort zone," the motivation disappears, and additional increases to efforts and results fall off. As a rule, the farther you move from a threat, the less motivation there is to move on. Managers, having seen the temporary success, often begin the process all over again. This sort of external "pushing" has only short-term effects on employee performance, but it can have long-term effects on your management style and coaching activities.

If you are a "pull" manager, you go to work thinking about the kinds of promises, rewards, and goals that will press your employees' "hot buttons." Again, you may have short-term success, but you also face the exhausting long-term project of thinking up new prizes. Once an external reward has been achieved, there will be no reason to increase effort and results. So the "pulling" manager has to keep pulling, setting up more, better, and always brighter prizes. That can't go on forever. The rule here is that the closer you move to the goal, the less motivation there is to go on.

"Pushing" and "pulling" managers supply external reinforcements, mistaking them for the *internal* motivations that produce long-term behavior. When reinforcements are purely *external* rewards or punishments, such "motivation" can have only a short-term effect. And as we have already observed, these reinforcements have an effect only on behavior—an effect that is always intermittent, as a manager can't be with an employee all the time. Reinforcements must be constantly renewed, if a desired behavior is to be constantly repeated.

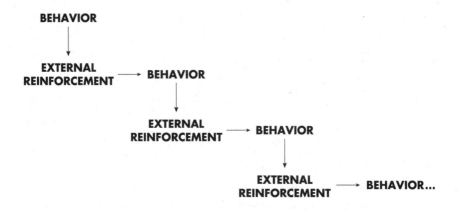

Figure 5.2
External Reinforcement

A constant input of reinforcements can sustain this sort of repetition indefinitely but does little to support or strengthen an individual's personal motivation.

In the long term, external "pushing" and "pulling" reinforce a whole range of unproductive attitudes and habits. Employees usually accept, and often *enjoy,* a "push" or a "pull." This is because most people are conditioned by upbringing and society to seek motivations and reinforcements *from others.* (A conditioning that is itself strongly reinforced: there are always plenty of people ready to tell us what to do and reward our compliance.) Many employees—those who are *not* self-managers—will be glad to relinquish their responsibility to you. From their point of view, it's like being coddled: someone is paying attention to them, telling them what to do, and cheering them on.

The effect of this coddling, however, is to send a message:

"Don't worry. You needn't take responsibility for your motivation: *we* will let you know when you have to work, how hard, and for how long." Such a message may have extremely damaging effects. It *creates* dependency—just what a manager needs to avoid. And when you promise somebody something for doing what they ought to be doing anyway, you run the risk that they will lose sight of the *real* reasons for doing it. There are also important consequences for the *manager.* If you become a skilled "motivator" (someone who can coax, deliver an effective pep talk, or pick out just the right size of carrot), you will get the job, and it can become a full-time job. Unfortunately, the paybacks are only part-time. Managers who "motivate" people can hope, at most, to *maintain* a level of performance and results. Increased growth and improved results are unlikely outcomes.

Internal "Push" and "Pull"

Constantly renewed external reinforcements *can* encourage the repetition of desired behavior, but it is by no means clear that the behavior can be called "habitual"; it is likely to be extinguished by the withdrawal of reinforcements. The coach must then complement the limitations of external reinforcements with a variety of strategies that will develop self-managing and self-reinforcing abilities. The role of the coach, of course, is to reinforce behaviors, but the real point is to develop and strengthen an individual's *self*-reinforcement and motivational systems.

External reinforcements quickly lose their power as we move away from the negative or approach the positive. Effective long-term motivation, then, depends on *internal* reinforcement. Unless people are allowed to find their own motivations within and encouraged to reinforce the efforts they undertake on their own initiative, managers will never be able to break out of the "carrot-and-stick" model of motivation. An external reinforcement is soon exhausted; another one must always be supplied. Internal reinforcement, however, *never stops.* It is truly said that "success breeds success": this is because a person's *feelings* of success and competence are never-ending and constantly reinforcing. Also, internal reinforcement, since it is continuous, has a more pronounced, long-term effect on motivation.

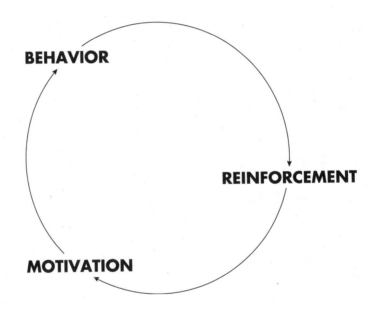

Figure 5.3
Internal Reinforcement

This self-sustaining cycle represents genuine habits of effort and thought, as opposed to a mere repetition of behavior that requires a constant input of external reinforcements.

"Push" and "Pull" Ratios

"Pull" and "push," when internalized, both drive sustained effort. We observed a classic example of the way both motivations work at a conference for leading sales representatives of a major financial services firm. One agent, during a discussion of motivation, admitted that he had just completed his most productive year, but he was concerned about how, and even whether, he could do it again next year. He admitted to great stress, some apprehension that he might not be able to repeat his success, and a lot of uncertainty about where large amounts of new business might be found. Another agent, equally successful, said that he too had just had his best year ever—but he felt great about it and was confident he could meet the challenge, and even exceed his performance, in the next year. Both were high performers, both were motivated to work, but one displayed the potentially limiting effects of "push" motivation, and the other the enabling influence of "pull" motivation.

Most people, however, need a combination of "pushes" and "pulls." And while each individual's motivational makeup is unique—varying to the same extent as individual psychology, upbringing, and circumstances—the best combinations generally favor "pull" motivation over "push." In fact, we believe that the ideal motivational mix is as little as 10% "push" and as much as 90% "pull," since "pull" motivations almost always involve less stress, better attitudes, and a higher degree of success. People motivated by a "push," after all, are essentially driven by *fear*, and they tend to keep looking back over their shoulder at whatever they are trying to escape. Those motivated by a "pull," however, keep looking forward to what they want to achieve, and because they are facing forward, they can see what lies beyond. The future orientation of "pull" motivation encourages sustained effort to reach an objective and is much more likely to lead to a sustained effort to reach one's goals.

The ideal 10%-90% ratio of "push" and "pull" passes through a kind of motivational breakthrough. At such a point, *avoidance,* along with all its negative associations, gives way to a positive *approach* towards a desirable condition.

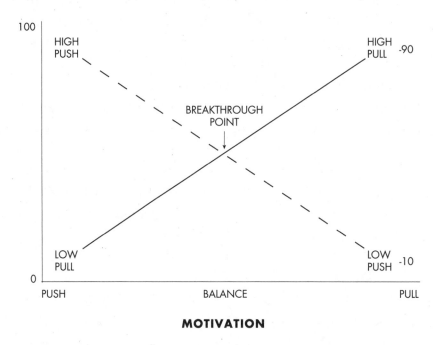

Figure 5.4
Approach and Avoidance: Breakthrough and Ideal Ratio

Creating a Self-Reinforcing Individual

As we have written, genuine motivations are *internal,* belonging solely to the employee, but managers are still held accountable for employees' *results.* What can managers do about employee motivation? We believe that this is a *coaching* issue. We have observed that effective coaches help people develop their own motivations. Often, managers find themselves *telling* people what to do, how to do it, and when to do it. In the hopes of "motivating" them, they also tell their people *why* they should do it—that is when the coaxing and cajoling begins. The best coaches, however, don't tell, they *ask.* They view their role as one of facilitating each person's attempts to set individual goals, and then consulting on the resources, reinforcement strategies, and efforts that will be needed to achieve those goals. Consider the following sequence of coaching questions as a means of helping an employee "go internal" to discover his or her own motivations. The sequence, which begins with the kind of results-oriented question you may have asked employees many times, keeps the focus on performance and sends an important message about responsibility:

- How do you feel about your results? Your performance?
- What do you want to accomplish? What are your goals?
- What do you think you need to do? Describe your action plan and the steps involved.
- What are you going to do?
- How will you self-reinforce it? How will you make it a *habit?*
- What help do you think you will need?
- Where can you get that help?

This sequence of questions appeals to internal motivations and is directed towards helping individuals define and achieve their success—not the large or abstract "success" that crowns a career or a lifetime of activity, but specific, concrete successes that can be enjoyed by the end of the day, week , or month. This success is crucial to self-motivation. The best—in fact, the only—long-term motivator of human performance is a sense of competency, of success.

The central concept is critical, the exact wording less so. What is essential is that the coaching questions place responsibility for motivation with the employee. The basic sequence is simple: "Where are you *now?* Where do you *want* to get? What do you need to *do? Will* you do it?" Initial questions must be kept wide open and non-specific. For example:

- How do you feel your year is going?
  is better than
- How do you feel about having no sales this week?

Being too specific, particularly about a negative point, tends to shut down the process. Asking people "Is something wrong?" or "Are you in trouble?" will just make them defensive—and they will almost always *deny* it. Starting with positives tends to reduce defensiveness. Still, open questions may not get an immediate answer; an employee may not have a ready response. Ask, wait, and listen.

Surprisingly, people may not have a ready answer for the second question about goals. Once again, patience and self-control are required. But it is also important to recognize that if there really is no internal goal, no personal desire or expectation, the rest of the coaching process will lead nowhere. If an employee needs more time, offer to suspend the discussion and take up the issue later, at a time the employee suggests. After all, it's *individuals'* motivation and commitment that you want to address, in addition to the goals and expectations that *you* may have for them.

If there is a goal, the third question discovers whether or not the individual has a game plan or a strategy for getting there. At this point a manager can play a consultant's role—being careful not to take ownership of the employee's plan. And the final question—"Will you do it?"—nails down the commitment. These specific efforts and activities will constitute a self-reinforcing habit. Unless these questions are asked—and answered—the process is an empty exercise. The questions are designed to identify positive expectations and determine whether the employee can *self-manage,* sourcing the necessary resources and coaching help.

Working through the coaching questions shifts the responsibility for motivation, strategy, commitment, effort, and, ultimately, performance from the manager to the individual. But note that these must be *genuine* questions. Managers may seem to ask questions ("Would you like to qualify for the conference?"), but employees may hear something quite different ("Work harder or you won't get to go"). Coaching questions must be asked in the course of an open, honest discussion, with no agenda on the manager's part, apart from encouraging the individual to think about these important questions.

The process has a surprisingly wide range of applications. We're always glad to hear success stories from the managers who use the approaches described in this book, but one story is particularly memorable. A young sales manager (we'll call him Fred) reported that he had used the coaching question process to get a new behavioral commitment from his ten-year-old daughter, a Grade Five student! As he told it,

"I was wondering whether the coaching for commitment process would be effective for my daughter. One day, I asked her, 'How's school going?' She said that it was fine and that she liked her teachers, and she told me about her good subjects. Then she added, 'But you know, Dad, I'm not doing well in math.'

"I said that I knew about that—and then I asked her, 'If you could accomplish anything you wanted in math this year, what would it be?' She said that she would be happy to get a B. So I asked her, 'What would you need to do to get a B?' She said she would probably have to start doing the math homework that she had tended to avoid. 'How could you manage that?', I asked. She said she should probably start doing her math homework first, even before watching TV. 'So,' I asked, 'Are you prepared to do that?' She said she was. I had a commitment from her, and it was surprisingly easy.

"The next night, I asked her how the math homework went; she said she had done it, and that it had been easier than she had expected. I congratulated her on keeping her commitment. I asked each night for a couple of weeks, providing positive reinforcement for the effort, and then, as time went on, once or twice a week. A few weeks after that, on an interim math test, she scored her best mark ever in math."

Fred facilitated the process beautifully—and the outcome was the most powerful motivation of all: his daughter's feelings of success and competence, both of which are fully internal.

Good coaches ask, and they also *listen.* The coaching question process may seem like a long and indirect way to "get people to do what you want," but that is not really a *coaching* goal. A coach acts as a partner in a common enterprise, assisting people to discover what has to be done and what a coach can't *tell* them. The coach proceeds on the understanding that people already know their goals and objectives, at least to some extent, and that they know best how they can work towards them. Coaches, then, stop *managing* (or "bossing") by encouraging employees to become *self*-managers who provide their own motivation. When you become a coach, you transfer the role of motivating to the individual, where, of course, it belongs. After all, motivating and reinforcing other people is *work* for you, but it's a natural, internal process for them.

BURN-OUT = A POOR RETURN

ON ENERGY

Chapter Six

MAXIMIZE RETURN ON ENERGY

Calculating Returns

Return on energy ("ROE") is, necessarily, a matter of *perceptions.* Although each individual feels that he or she knows "how much" energy has been invested in an activity, the judgement is really a *qualitative* one; there is no scale or measure that can be applied. As a result, it is very common for people to feel shortchanged on their effort if they focus exclusively on *quantitative,* results-based, external reinforcement. At a very basic level, there can be no rational proportion between a person's subjective, qualitative evaluation of the energy he or she expends and other people's objective, quantitative evaluations of the results that are produced. The two are categorically distinct. It is not surprising, then, that a person with a strong conviction that his or her work is important may endure setbacks and what others take to be failures, or that a very well-paid employee may nevertheless feel unsatisfied or unappreciated.

A poor perceived return on energy, then, is the result of an internal process. If the external reinforcements, predicated on the results, are the only measurement, effort may or may *not* seem to have been rewarded. When *internal* reinforcements are also taken into consideration, the returns can be substantially increased. This sort of calculation must be made by the individual. No one else knows the precise quality of effort involved, and no one else can provide the personal satisfaction, the sense of integrity and accomplishment, that is the best payback for good effort. A coaching manager, recognizing the private, internal nature of this process, does not attempt to "do it all." Instead, the coach helps employees focus on their own efforts and their results, first, to reinforce the implied effort and the obvious results, and second, to validate the employee's *own process of assessing ROE.*

Returns on Energy

R > E

When returns are perceived as exceeding energy, attitudes and expectations are strengthened and progress seems much more likely. Even when the difference between energy and returns is small, the effect on confidence and conviction can be significant. A high level of satisfaction reinforces our efforts and urges us on to make new gains. We feel that we are "on a roll" and, in the long run, the small advances, like interest, begin to compound.

R = E

When returns are seen to be more or less equally balanced with the energy invested, attitudes are not so deeply affected. Nevertheless, attitudes are fragile: little things can easily disturb them, and we tend to move tentatively, on a day-to-day basis. Investments are made, after all, in the hope of gains. When the returns just offset the investment, there may be less encouragement to persevere, and we may consider directing our efforts elsewhere. (People don't usually stick with a mutual fund, for example, just because it isn't *losing* money.) The best we can expect from such situations is to maintain the status quo.

R < E

A poor perceived return on energy is the first symptom of job dissatisfaction, frustration, and burn-out. It has an immediate effect on attitudes. When we think we are getting less out of an activity than we are putting in, we are likely to question our expectations, our motives, our circumstances, and perhaps even the value of the whole enterprise. These negative attitudes tend to accelerate the process of burn-out to the point where we may give up trying altogether.

The Manager's ROE

As we have noted, some managers spend most of their time and energy dealing with *poor* performers. Where the results are poor, there must be a problem, and it is the conventional manager's job to solve it by "motivating" the employee, looking for new approaches and techniques, supplying training, going over past performance, delivering pep talks, and so on. While good performers may get little more than a quick "way to go," poor performers tend to get a lot of detailed "please go and...." Sometimes this happens because managers are mandated by the organization to spend equal time with everybody—and then find themselves taking even longer with the people who seem to need it most. But when this happens, who seems to be more important? Who is getting most of the manager's attention? And what does the manager get in return?

In choosing your management strategies, consider again the two basic factors in performance—effort and talent—and the way these are mapped against results (see Figure 6.1).

Then consider where you allocate your time and effort. Are they consistently devoted to the areas that are getting the best results and showing the best efforts? There is a simple way to be sure that you get a *good* return on your energy:

1. Concentrate your time and attention on the employees who get good results and those who work hard. Use this time to

a) help them find strengths and growth opportunities, and arrange for the necessary resources.

b) find out what they can do, what they are willing to do, and what they will do—and hold them to it.

c) reinforce their efforts and encourage them to set higher levels of expectation.

d) listen to their suggestions and ideas about the work they do and the goals they set for themselves.

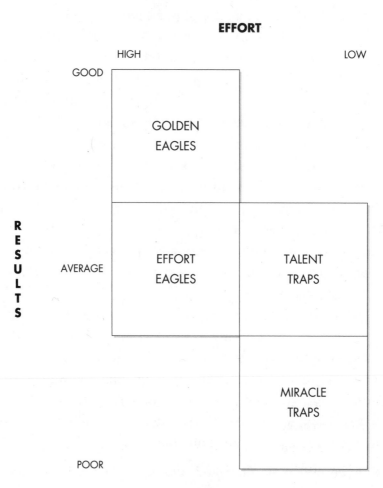

Figure 6.1
Effort and Results

2. Reduce the amount of time and effort you give to talented employees who just won't work hard on their own, and to low-talent, low-effort employees:

   a) Let them know that while the occasional good result lets them keep their job, only effort will win your support for their careers.

   b) Make it clear that you offer your help in exchange for making commitments and keeping them.

   c) Keep discussions and reviews to a minimum, and avoid joint projects in which you are supposed to set an example.

   d) Make sure they are aware that there is a minimum workload or quota they must achieve to retain their position. Make sure they are attaining that level; then look for your best results *elsewhere,* with the people who can get them.

Compare this coaching approach with a two-step recipe for getting a *poor* return on your energy:

1. Spend lots of time and effort on the employees who don't work hard. Use this time to

   a) retrain them, teaching them what they already know.

   b) coax, cajole, and pep-talk them into working harder.

   c) go to work with them to demonstrate a full day's work effort.

   d) listen to their complaints about what's wrong with _____ (choose any of the following: the product, the company, the system, the pay, the economy, the territory).

2. Leave the effort employees *alone*—or

   a) congratulate them and give them a pat on the back every now and then.

   b) ask for their help.

c) cancel or postpone reviews, discussions, and joint projects.

d) arbitrarily increase their quotas and/or workload.

These two steps let the non-effort employees know that you think they are important, deserving of your time and energy, and that they are safe in your system. And rest assured that *nothing will change.* (Except you will be feeling increasingly stressed and under-appreciated, and if your team's results are not yet hurting you, they soon will be.) Your high-effort people will eventually start to feel shortchanged and may eventually begin to look elsewhere for what they need.

You can maximize your ROE, then, by refusing to coax, and coaching on the basis of effort *and* results. If the effort was not expended, ten seconds might be enough time to make it clear to an employee that there is nothing to discuss. If the effort was expended, the manager can spend time acknowledging the effort, confirming the employee's sense that he or she tried hard, and planning ways to get more or better results out of that hard work. And appropriate time can also be spent with the people who make a good effort *and* get good results—those people have plenty of potential, and a small increase in skill or knowledge can bring big increases in results.

Poor performance and unsatisfactory results are, of course, a problem, but not a problem that you *alone* can solve. You may, with the best intentions, make yourself responsible for your employees' performance. But when you do, you prevent them from taking responsibility, and you reinforce their dependency on external direction and reinforcement. You are also likely to be exhausted by the effort of doing *their* jobs as well as your own, and therefore have less energy than may be required to do any of the jobs well. When you focus on coaching the better performers, the poor performers will learn where your time and energy are going, and some will make an attempt to earn it. When they do, they will be embarking on the path to self-management, keeping commitments to effort and getting coaching from you.

You get the best returns on your own time and energy, then, when you invest them in good performers, and, in the long run, you will also get the best results from your good performers. When you boost your own ROE, you are taking a direct, practical step to prevent burn-out, a critical issue for every manager. Working with high-performance and high-potential people has both short- and long-term benefits. From the very outset, you will be directing experience and energy towards the people who appreciate them the most and who will make the best use of them. Ask any manager what it's like to spend a day in the field with a top performer: typical responses are "An enjoyable day!" and "The time went so quickly!" Ask the same question about poor performers, and the answers range from "A long day" to "Pure drudgery." When you concentrate on coaching your high-performance and high-potential people, you will be withdrawing your time and effort from those who make the heaviest demands and yet profit the least from your attention. Burn-out is unlikely when you deliberately invest your energy in activities that have the best potential for returns. And in the long term, this prudent "investment strategy" will make for both personal and professional success.

The Employee's ROE

Enjoying a sense of worthwhile effort, as well as (or even in spite of) the results, is an important self-management strategy. It is crucial, then, for self-managers, and for the coaches who want to develop them, to break loose from a routine dependency on external reinforcements. Managers might be able to improve employees' ROE by trying to *increase* the returns, but the effects would be short-lived, and the managers would find themselves trapped in a never-ending cycle of incentives. Coaching strategies, in contrast, target these dependencies and offer alternatives. A coach can help employees *recognize* all the returns that are available to them, internal as well as external.

EXTERNAL FACTORS	INTERNAL FACTORS
REWARDS	SATISFACTION
PUNISHMENT	POSITIVE SELF-EVALUATION
PAYOFFS	SENSE OF ACCOMPLISHMENT
CONGRATULATIONS	SENSE OF SUCCESS
PRAISE	SENSE OF COMPLETION

Figure 6.2
ROE Factors

The first step is to acknowledge people's efforts, as well as the results they produce. This may be a challenge. Coaches don't have to make qualitative judgments of character and performance: they apply a simple quantitative system based on effort and results. In this way, they can show an appreciation of effort and, more importantly, confirm a person's own internal sense of satisfaction or achievement. Coaches can't actually provide others with internal reinforcement, but they can encourage them to develop and strengthen processes of self-reinforcement that are already in place.

SET OBJECTIVES, MEASURE RESULTS,

MANAGE BY EFFORT.

Chapter Seven

MANAGE BY EFFORT

Most managers have experienced the tension between *objectives* (the goals that have to be met) and *results* (the outcomes that are achieved). And many managers are aware that they spend much of their time worrying about one or the other of the two. Either you are looking *forward* to something that hasn't happened, but that you want to make happen, or you are looking *back,* evaluating and auditing whatever has already happened and can't be changed. Given these competing distractions, it's no wonder that we sometimes neglect an important point—that there is only one way to move from objectives to results, and that is through consistent daily effort.

Managers may also neglect the critical role of effort when, for any number of reasons, objectives and results are well-matched. When this happens, everyone is in the "comfort zone": managers are reinforced and well-compensated, and whatever problems exist seem less urgent. It is worth noting, however, that there may be little stability or security in such a situation. Progress is made day by day, month by month, or quarter by quarter. There is no long-term perspective on goals and successes, largely because there is little examination of the process that connects objectives and results. When results are satisfactory and results are all that count, people often fail to ask *why* or *how* the results were achieved. Consequently, there is little development of conscious competence. They miss the opportunity to learn or to build on strengths and to move quickly from acceptable results to even better results.

Typically, a circumstantial match between objectives and

results seldom lasts for long. Usually the relationship varies from day to day or week to week. Sometimes it is possible to coast on good results, only to discover suddenly that a shortfall requires a special effort to "catch up." Most people are familiar with the rollercoaster effect that follows: when every peak is followed by a trough, you finally stop thinking about where you are going and just try to hold on.

Good coaches, however, prefer to explore and analyze their successes. There is nothing like a winning streak to create an opportunity for the coach to devise strategies to develop potential. When a team is winning or has had a string of successes, everyone is "on a high" and open to strategies for improvement. So, when objectives and results match up, effective managers are glad to reinforce the success, but they also see the success as an opportunity to build on strengths. They attempt to "raise the bar," identifying the factors that led to the achievement and developing them, so as to improve performance and, subsequently, results. When approached systematically, results can be improved by improving the process.

Managing by Objectives and Results

Managers of every kind must, of course, deal with objectives and results: that is the nature of business. A variety of management models have attempted to make a virtue of that necessity. In the 1970s, "management by objectives" (MBO) was widely popularized as a solution to productivity issues; in the 1980s, "management by results" (MBR) was extolled as a means to motivate employees and to achieve targets and quotas. Neither MBO nor MBR is, strictly speaking, a management *system*. Both are generalized approaches to management that emphasize just one of the important parts of the coaching process to establish criteria for performance.

If the results measure up to or exceed the objectives, both MBO and MBR tend to maintain the status quo. As long as the objectives are met, there will be little analysis of how and why the results were achieved. But when the results do *not* reach the objectives, both approaches become MBC—management by *crisis.* A discrepancy between objectives and results is usually unexpected and has the character of a catastrophe. In the MBC model, time and energy are used to react to the crisis; every effort is an effort to *compensate* or *catch up.* Managing by crisis necessarily takes very short-term views; there is little time or energy left to make plans or form long-range goals. Crisis management is essentially a *reaction* to circumstances, and the reaction typically takes the form of the dreaded "Why?" "Why weren't the objectives achieved?" "Why weren't the results good enough?" These are not bad questions. The problem is finding good answers.

The Dreaded "Why?"

As a manager, you probably learned very quickly the futility of asking "Why?" whenever an employee failed to achieve a positive outcome or a desired result. That's because the typical response is a series of excuses or rationalizations to "explain" the failure. When the *real* problem "occurs as a process"—due to improper preparation, ineffective procedures, or poor effort—it is futile to discuss the excuses. It wastes time, and it doesn't really change what you would do another time. There's no real way to respond effectively to the typical excuses that managers routinely encounter when they ask "Why?" after the results are in. Asking the dreaded "Why?" is generally counter-productive, in that it allows, even asks, the employee to offer excuses that, once uttered, sound more relevant and compelling than ever. The time a manager spends listening, rebuking, accepting, objecting, or responding in any way reinforces both the excuses and the employee's lack of effort. Remember, anything on which a manager spends time or energy is *strengthened.* That is why it is crucial to allocate your time and energy strategically.

If you do slip and find yourself asking the dreaded "Why?", wait for the employee to finish, but don't respond or acknowledge when you know you are just getting excuses that rationalize a lack of effort. Rather than ask "Why?", ask direct, specific questions. Go back to the controllables, and go back to commitments:

- How did the activities and efforts go?
- How well did you execute them?
- What do you see as your next step?

Presumably, we ask the dreaded "Why" so that we can learn from our mistakes. But, as we have already noted, this sort of learning provides very little to apply to our next efforts. Conscious incompetence is an important part of our self-understanding; it helps to know what to avoid, and it also creates a growth opportunity. However, conscious competence is even more important. It is always better to know what worked and do that more often.

Managing by crisis, then, goes the wrong way on a one-way street:

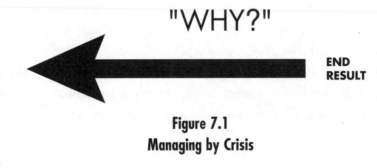

Figure 7.1
Managing by Crisis

Energy and attention are wasted in after-the-fact analyses, endless re-examinations of past events, rationalizations, and excuses. If an effort has been unproductive or unsuccessful, resolve not to do it again, and move on at once.

MBO and MBR can become crisis management, because results, at some point, may fail to meet objectives. The real problem is that both MBO and MBR overlook the *process* that is the controllable aspect of performance. When uncontrollables surface, they are not recognized as such. They make themselves known indirectly, in excuses and rationalizations. Employees are often very creative when making excuses, and managers are impressed with the creativity. Excuses have some value, but only as evidence of barriers, obstacles, and surprises that couldn't be anticipated or overcome. In a crisis mode, MBO and MBR focus only on uncontrollables. As a result, responsibility for performance and the controllables can be overlooked.

Coaching the Process

Managing by *effort* (MBE) focuses on the process and builds on the controllables. MBE makes no attempt to control the uncontrollables: nothing wastes more energy more quickly. Instead, attention and energy are redirected to the controllable aspects of *performance,* where they can make a real difference. There is only one way to get from objectives to results, after all, and that is through consistent, effective effort. Identifying the controllables saves energy, energy that can be used productively throughout a process that links objectives and results.

It is crucial for a coach to recognize this *process,* the performance that is determined by effort, attitude, and opportunity. Coaches look for a *series* of initiatives and outcomes, and make a distinction between a number of interim steps or "process results" and the end result. In this series, it is possible to see how well things are going long before the final result is in. Throughout the process, it is possible to evaluate and coach performance. The manager employing the MBR approach has to wait until the end of the process, at which point he or she can only reinforce (reward or punish) the result. This is a bit like trying to manage history.

OBJECTIVES $\rightarrow$ EFFORT $\rightarrow$ $R_1 \rightarrow R_2 \rightarrow R_3 \rightarrow R_4 \rightarrow$ END RESULT

	MANAGEMENT BY EFFORT	
10%	$\longleftarrow$ —————— 80% —————— $\longrightarrow$	10%

Figure 7.2
From Objectives to Results

As Figure 7.2 suggests, objectives and results are an essential part of the management system. Objectives and results, while necessary to the process, cannot be managed or coached. Goal-setting is a crucial process for coaches and their people, as it sets the direction for the process. After all, "If you don't know where you are going, any road will take you there." Goal-setting provides a concrete target; it posits the results that must be achieved to fully enjoy a success. The coach begins by working with the employee to set objectives and moves on as soon as possible to the actual effort. Developing objectives in partnership is a powerful motivating strategy. An imposed quota, in contrast, seems at best like homework and at worst like a punishment. But objectives that are negotiated with the employee and committed to by the employee are *personal* goals. As a rule, people have more commitment to what they create. It is also important to remember that the most useful objectives not only anticipate a certain desired result but also set out a series of specific, well-devised efforts that will lead to the result. Rather than one final result, the coach looks at the series of interim steps. A good coach helps an employee combine a single, long-term objective with a number of interim initiatives.

Results, of course, are essential. You must know what you have accomplished! And results are needed as a basis for compensation and financial administration, to track the ongoing health of the organization, and to chart the success of your team. But identifying a wider range of "process results" increases the utility of results-oriented evaluations. Such results provide the employee and coach with the information needed to guide coaching and learning within the process.

The largest part of the process, the 80%, consists of the series of interim steps and outcomes. It is here that the most effective coaching takes place. At every point in the process, good coaches can make a difference, by providing appropriate advice and consulting—and by asking the right questions, so that the employee can self-evaluate his or her proficiency and effectiveness at each step. Coaches are careful not to demand *more* effort: while they know that effort levels can be adjusted, they realize that asking people to "try harder" is coaxing, not coaching. Instead, they facilitate increased commitments to effort or suggest ways to direct effort more effectively, so as to build on strengths and maximize returns on energy. There are four basic ways to improve performance and maximize results:

1. Working more consistently.
2. Working harder.
3. Working smarter.
4. Working harder and smarter.

1. Working more consistently

This is the easiest way, as you keep on doing what you are doing, only on a more regular and predictable basis. If, for example, you make an average of a hundred sales calls a week, you are likely to be better prepared and more effective if you schedule twenty calls each day, rather than try to get through all of them at the beginning of the week (or let them accumulate until the end of the week). Performance and results can improve with minimal extra effort, directly improving your ROE as well.

2. Working harder

Performance can also be improved by applying extra effort. Again, you continue to do what you have been doing, but you increase the quantity of your effort. For example, you might raise your weekly quota of sales calls to 120. That's just another four calls a day, but a whole extra day's work added to your weekly performance. Working harder is likely to improve performance and results more than simply working consistently. That's important, since you will want to feel that you are getting a good return on the extra effort that you are investing in the job.

3. Working smarter

A more challenging approach is to continue doing what you are doing well, but add and/or modify activities that will improve performance by changing the quality of your effort. For instance, you might develop a screening process that helps you identify high-potential clients, and develop selling techniques that address their specific circumstances and needs. Even if you continue to make the same number of calls, the extra effort you make to target your clients can help you get better results.

4. Working harder and smarter

The most difficult method of improving performance—but the one with the greatest potential for impressive improvement—is to improve both the quantity and quality of effort. Starting with what you do well, doing it more, and then doing it better takes plenty of extra effort, but it offers the best chance of steady improvement and increasingly good results—all of which, in turn, will reinforce your self-confidence and growth.

At the end of the process, it is essential to review the final result, as well as the "process" results that preceded it. Good coaching does not just compare objectives and results to draw simple conclusions about success or failure, or to calculate the appropriate reinforcement; rather, the assessment is part of an integrated system that includes the process. Results do count, and a good coach takes them into consideration when evaluating and reinforcing the performance that produced them.

The importance of the process was powerfully underscored at a meeting of sales personnel for a multinational company. There were a few experienced agents and quite a few new hires. Their top agent was asked, "Bert, can you guarantee a sale today?" His answer—"No"—was immediate and caused a certain amount of consternation among the newer reps. If their top producer couldn't be sure of getting a sale, how could they ever hope to succeed? Bert was asked, "Why not?", and his explanation is worth recalling on a daily basis: "Somebody *else* decides that." Then he was asked, "Can you guarantee to contact ten prospects today?" "Absolutely," was the reply. The initial effort was completely within his control—something the rookies, focusing on *results,* might have forgotten.

In a way, the choice is simple. If you want to apply pressure on your people, manage by results. And up to a point, that may be your best strategy. All that talent traps (and, on rare occasions, miracle traps) have to show is the results they get, and with these employees, that is all you need to look at—for as long as it takes to make the point that you are concerned about effort and performance too. However, if you want to stimulate the rest of your people—but without so much pressure as to inhibit performance—then talk to them about the front end of the process, the controllables. Ask them to make commitments to the controllables (that is, to efforts) and expect them to keep those commitments.

Performance Evaluation

Performance evaluation is one of a manager's most important tasks. It can also be one of the most difficult, but many managers are tempted to take a shortcut, simply equating an employee's performance with the results he or she achieves. It's not surprising that most evaluations are made on the basis of results or outcomes. They are *objective* and measurable; they allow quick and easy comparisons among employees; they provide reliable evidence that can be used to defend a manager's assessment of an employee's value to an organization and its interests.

To coach effectively, then, managers must teach their trainees to recognize and assess the controllable elements of any job or process:

1. The preparation: "Was I prepared to the extent that I felt confident and in control?"
2. The execution (effort): "How skillful was my performance of the steps in the process?"
3. The result (outcome): "What did I achieve?"

Figure 7.3
Preparation, Execution, and Results

The challenge is to evaluate each stage independently of the others. Preparation precedes execution, and both precede and help to determine results. Our assessments, however, often reverse the sequence: we start by considering the results and then judge the preparation and execution accordingly. If the results are good, it is easy to simply assume that preparation and execution were well-developed. Closer analysis, however, conducted on each step in turn, may indicate otherwise.

When each phase is evaluated independently, performance evaluations can provide a detailed picture of people's strengths and areas for development, and specific estimates of their potential for effort and achievement. Such evaluations are learning opportunities, not just "report cards." They help develop conscious competence, as well as conscious incompetence, by addressing the controllable aspects of performance. The evaluations bear directly on things that employees can work on and encourage them to take responsibility for improvements.

Benefits of Coaching

The managing effort system differs in many respects from other managerial approaches. As the discussions in Chapters Three to Seven have shown, coaching involves a shift in orientation and emphasis (see Figure 7.4).

The benefits are obvious, both for you and for your employees. When you allow your people to take responsibility and encourage them to manage their own objectives, efforts, and accomplishments, you create an environment that is less stressful and more productive. Job satisfaction increases, performance improves, and, in the long run, you get the improved *results* for which you, as a manager, are accountable.

MANAGER	→ COACH
FOCUS ON RESULTS	→ FOCUS ON EFFORT
COAXING	→ COACHING
TELLING	→ ASKING
CONTROLLING	→ GUIDING
GIVING ORDERS AND DIRECTIONS	→ FACILITATING INITIATIVES AND GOALS
FORCING COMPLIANCE	→ GETTING COMMITMENT
PROVIDING EXTERNAL REINFORCEMENT	→ ENCOURAGING A BALANCE OF EXTERNAL REINFORCEMENT AND SELF-REINFORCEMENT
MANAGING BY RESULTS	→ MANAGING BY EFFORT AND RESULTS
SUPPORTING PEOPLE	→ SUPPORTING PEOPLE'S EFFORTS
"MOTIVATING"	→ FACILITATING SELF-MOTIVATION

Figure 7.4
Changing Orientations

When you coach people to get the job done and then help them find ways to do it better, you will be doing your *own* job, and that means more job satisfaction for you. Managers who spend all their time and energy on poor performers, trying to bring them up to speed or compensating for their shortfalls, soon find themselves exhausted, their resources depleted. With the best of intentions, they burn themselves out. But coaches can avoid burn-out. They try to develop self-managers, and they are self-managers themselves: they know their strengths and manage their efforts to achieve their goals. Like all self-managers, coaches know how much they can do, and they do it. The satisfaction of doing that, day after day, reinforces self-confidence and constantly resets expectations for more and better performance.

CREATING A SELF-MANAGEMENT SYSTEM:

1. DETERMINE THE ESSENTIALS.

2. ESTABLISH AN ADMISSION TICKET.

3. REINFORCE THE ESSENTIALS.

Chapter Eight

CREATING A SELF-MANAGEMENT SYSTEM: STEP ONE

Three Steps to a Self-Management System

In Chapters Eight to Ten, we describe the practical, day-to-day process that you can use to recognize good performance, encourage good potential, and develop the initiative and ability of your people. Drawing on the concepts and strategies explored in preceding chapters, we will set out three basic steps to take in developing and sustaining a self-management system:

1. Determine the "essentials."
2. Establish an admission ticket for your time.
3. Reinforce the essentials and the results, and train self-reinforcement.

The process is directly practical, in that it builds on *existing* strengths. Its success doesn't depend on starting with a "clean slate" or making a complete break with the past. The goal is to develop the positive potential of *any* given set of circumstances. So the process doesn't require any sweeping reorganization of established procedures, working conditions, or the people you already have in place. The focus is not on these externals—luckily, for managers can rarely change them. If they could, it would be easy to *solve* management "problems." The process we describe acknowledges the fact that management challenges— and opportunities—arise in the less-than-ideal circumstances in which pretty well everyone lives and works.

Ideal conditions are not required, then, and neither are

radical external changes. But the process does require what may strike you as a radical change in the way you respond to circumstances and manage externals. The development of a self-management system begins with a clear-sighted assessment of your workplace, your people, and yourself, with a view to determining what works best in your organization—and why. Then, rather than exclusively trying to "solve problems" or "fix things," you can use effective, day-by-day coaching techniques to promote and extend good potential, good efforts, and, of course, good results. The long-range objective is to create a largely self-sustaining process of constant improvement—but your daily responsibility is to facilitate, encourage, and reinforce your people's self-management abilities. And your first task is to determine the best way for them to exhibit those abilities.

"You Need to Know What You Need to Do"

The first step in establishing a self-management system is to determine the key activities and behaviors that produce the results your employees need and want. In every job or occupation, there are certain steps, actions, or processes that are essential to the accomplishment of specific goals. Sometimes these are referred to as "best practices." We'll just call them "the essentials"—the activities and behaviors that are consistently associated with good efforts, valuable performance, and satisfying results.

The Essentials

As an effective manager, your principal interest is not novel ways of doing things but established ways of doing things well: effective actions that produce the right results. Good, productive activity is no doubt taking place in your department, but with many employees, it's on an inconsistent basis.

Creating a self-management system begins, then, with identifying these essentials—the necessary behaviors and activities—in your department, organization, industry, or business. To identify the essentials, the question is, "What are the behaviors that would virtually guarantee the success of a person working in this or that position?" It is important to stress that you are looking for controllable *behavior*—specific, concrete activities and processes that are associated with high performance, good results, and personal and professional success. When identifying the essentials, there is no need to try to get "inside" a good performer's psychology. All that is required is knowing what behaviors are central to good performance and results. So, for example, you might observe that a top-performing customer service rep always makes a follow-up call two days after delivery of the product and checks back again a week later. This behavior is related to the more abstract attributes of positive relationship-building and follow-up. However, it is what the service rep actually does, in a regular and consistent fashion, that produces the results.

The essentials can be investigated according to the model shown in Figure 8.1. Every attitude and behavior, whether directly observable or, at this stage, simply desirable, can be classified, and the appropriate action taken.

Some attitudes and behaviors will be obviously good or bad. Others, however, may be more difficult to assess, since they may be more or less valuable in given circumstances. An aggressive, "go get 'em" attitude, for example, is fine in a sales environment where there will be only one sale to a client and where no follow-up is expected. But in a situation where repeat clients are developed and follow-up is paramount, that attitude could be a problem. The evaluation tool shown in Figure 8.1 can help fine-tune your assessments of the activities and attributes that your people need to do well.

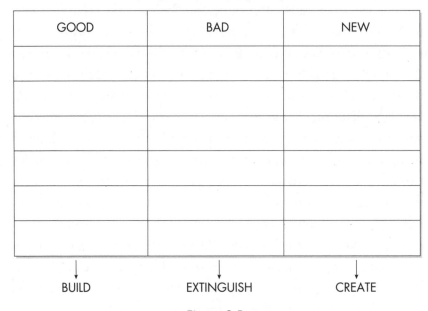

Figure 8.1
Identifying Essentials

There is, to some extent, a tradeoff between the direct value of a behavior or attitude and the degree of competence (skills, knowledge, or just plain "smarts") and consistency (constant and perhaps strenuous effort) that it involves. Obviously, low-value activities that require high levels of competence ought to be avoided, while high-value behaviors that require little competence (when they are available!) are top priorities. In between, however, are a variety of procedures that must be considered with careful attention to the specific circumstances.

As a manager with experience, you probably have a very good idea of what critical behaviors are essential to good performance in your business. In fact, you probably demonstrated most, if not all, of these behaviors during the early training of your employees. These behaviors are specific, definable activities. They include such things as the type of preparation or preplanning and start times. If you are a sales manager, they also include making a certain number of calls and following the steps of a well-defined sales process. When you train people in the essentials, you are providing them with the means to perform well and get good results, which is the first step towards a fully developed self-management system.

One of the key reasons you were selected to be a manager may be the fact that you know how to do the job that the people you manage and coach have to do. But if that is the case, you have probably found out that telling and showing them what to do is seldom enough to ensure that they do it regularly and consistently. Or perhaps you don't have any on-the-job experience that qualifies you to step in and take over the jobs your people do. That's quite all right—you don't need it. It's not your job to do their job! In a self-management system, you don't have to know exactly what your people ought to do and tell them to do it; you have to know how to ask what they ought to be doing, and you have to know how to *hear* what they are saying. In some ways, it's an advantage when you *aren't* the "expert." Then, instead of competing with your employee ("I could do this myself, but how are you going handle it?"), you can offer your own managerial expertise ("What are you going to do, and what will make it happen?").

ESTABLISH AN ADMISSION TICKET.

Chapter Nine

CREATING A SELF-MANAGEMENT SYSTEM: STEP TWO

Commitment and Compliance

The distinction between commitment and compliance is crucial to effective coaching. The differences are many, but easily summed up:

> The top-down approach to management typically *demands* compliance and may get it, for a while.

> The self-management approach *asks* people to make commitments and then holds them accountable.

Compliance is doing what you are told. It requires only that you meet an externally imposed standard for behavior or activity. Typically, this standard establishes the minimum requirements for a "satisfactory" performance, so compliance is also doing *just* what you are told and no more.

Compliance is related to position and power. To get compliance from others, you tell them what to do and typically back up your demand with some kind of power or authority. This may succeed for a number of reasons. First, many people are conditioned to accept direction. The demand for compliance is supported by authority, title or position, appeals to previous conditioning involving authority figures, and a dependence on external management. This demand is typically strengthened by the promise of pleasant consequences or the threat of unpleasant consequences and is enforced by means of supervision.

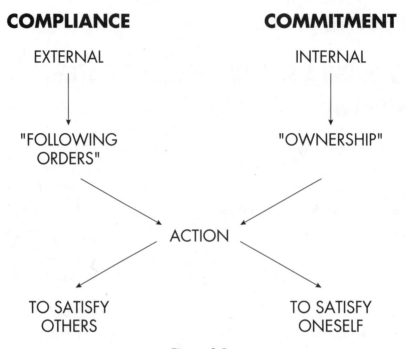

Figure 9.1
Compliance and Commitment

Compliance, however, seldom leads to any long-term behavioral change, as it depends on having an authority figure constantly monitor behavior and manage performance. When people comply with external demands, they tend to expend their effort as efficiently as possible, doing only as much as they *have* to do to make the grade. If sales managers, for example, demand that every sales rep make 50 sales calls each week, they may get that level of performance, but they seldom get *any* more. (And they may have to wonder whether the 50 calls listed are genuine calls.) The imposed quota ("what you *must* do") rather than individual potential ("what you *will* do") becomes the criterion of success, the expectation.

Ironically, the manager who demands compliance is usually the person who expends the most effort. Such a manager, after all, takes on responsibility for the entire process: setting the objective, determining the required activities, coaxing or compelling people to perform them, supervising their efforts, evaluating their results, keeping them on track, and making good any shortfalls (while extending attention to every aspect of a job that does not fall within his or her range.) Then, at the end of the week, month, or quarter, the manager must set the whole process in motion once again. The tasks of constantly supplying quantitative reinforcement and constantly structuring the environment will likely overburden conscientious managers. It's hard to imagine that the returns, however high, will reward that sort of investment, and so burn-out is more or less inevitable. And on the way to burn-out, this heavy-handed, top-down style of management will also dampen creativity, reduce overall expectations, and curb the development of self-managers.

The most effective way to achieve long-term behavioral change is to have people make their own commitments. Gaining commitment involves helping an individual select his or her own standard. The *individual* must identify, based on a knowledge of the business and the training previously received, what he or she needs to do and make a personal decision to do it. Gaining commitment from others involves asking them about, and allowing them to make, their own choices and decisions. Attempting to coerce performance and take all the responsibility (an approach to management that many would now call traditional or old-fashioned) may have the benefits of clear expectations, speed, and directness, but they are more than offset by the decrease in effectiveness.

The Benefits of Commitment

The benefits of commitment can be appreciated by considering the overall value of any initiative or strategy as the mathematical product of its *quality* and the *commitment* people bring to it. Even the best plan (ten out of ten on a quality scale) can fail if the person on whom the plan relies has a low level of commitment. Consider a case in which one of your employees is underachieving. You may have responded by devising a plan to turn things around, presenting it to the employee as the "solution" to a "problem." If you have ever done this, consider the strategy or plan you devised: on a scale of one to ten, how would you rate it? Since it was based on your knowledge and experience, it was probably a pretty good plan—let's say a nine. Now, given your experience as a manager, what level of commitment is an underachieving employee likely to bring to the implementation of your plan? Most managers suggest a "2" or a "3."

PLAN QUALITY	X	PLAN COMMITMENT	=	RESULTS
9	X	3	=	27

Figure 9.2
Low Commitment

Only when both components have high scores individually are the best overall values achieved. A high level of commitment can even redeem an ordinary or merely acceptable plan. The poorly performing employee, for example, may not have as much experience to draw on as the manager, but if he is allowed to make his *own* plan, the strong commitment he will bring to it can compensate.

PLAN QUALITY	X	PLAN COMMITMENT	=	RESULTS
6	X	9	=	54

Figure 9.3
High Commitment

Even better results become possible when a well-developed coaching system is used to help the employee develop improved initiatives. As the plan quality improves, coming eventually to equal the plan commitment, the best results begin to emerge.

PLAN QUALITY	X	PLAN COMMITMENT	=	RESULTS
9	X	9	=	81

Figure 9.4
Optimal Conditions

Gaining Commitments

The key to gaining commitment is to realize that it comes, by definition, from the individual. A decision must be made internally to qualify as a commitment. It sounds like "I will." Compliance, on the other hand, is determined by an external force. It may sound like "I must" or "I should," but this is really no more than a kind of echo, an internalization of someone else's "*you* must." Compliance may be required by the law, the rule book, a parent, or a boss, but in every case it comes from outside the individual.

Compliance occurs when someone tells people what to do and then orders them to do it. Commitment occurs when an *individual* makes his or her own decision about what to do. And while compliance usually requires some form of external influence, power, authority, or expertise, commitment requires *just one person.* The challenge for the manager, then, is to have employees decide to work hard with increasing expectations and, at the same time, avoid *telling* or *ordering* them to do so. The challenge is to gain commitment, rather than compliance.

Since commitment cannot be driven or forced from the outside, it is clear that gaining commitment from others requires their full involvement in the process. Although this is evident, many people in authority fail to appreciate the critical importance of *gaining commitment* to behavioral change, and they continue, with all good intentions, to tell people what to do.

If we accept that developing self-managers is the key role of managing, then facilitating the making of commitments (and expecting them to be kept) is perhaps the most important of all management responsibilities. This process lets people have responsibility; it allows them ownership. It also lets the coach learn early on about the self-management potential of the individual.

It has been said that making and keeping a commitment to an action or activity that takes one toward the achievement of a goal is the genuine source of personal power and, therefore, one of the best things people can do for their self-esteem. The benefits are many. Most importantly, people who make and keep their commitments become capable of self-directed and self-sustaining growth. They no longer need an authority or a manager to set their goals or explain the way to achieve them. A good coach will look for opportunities to help this happen and will then build on the new behavior to facilitate increased commitments or effort—all in the best interests of the individual being coached.

When this approach to gaining commitment is first suggested to managers in actual business situations, their intuitive response is often one of concern. Will the employees come up with the right level of commitment or even the right commitment? This concern is only natural, since the manager's welfare and success are directly related to the success of his or her people. This connection makes it difficult to exercise the patience and self-control necessary to ask for, listen to, wait for, and avoid judging the commitment.

It's Their Commitment

When people make commitments, they are expressing a sense of ownership. Coaches are careful to differentiate between the *making* of a commitment and the *quality* of a commitment. The former is always a good thing and must always be reinforced. The latter, however, may be open to question. But a good coach is very careful about how he or she comments on the quality of the plan. Using your position to judge people's commitments violates their sense of ownership. To make that sort of judgment is to take it away from them and subject it to an external standard. Judgments can destroy commitments, even, to some extent, when they are favorable. If the manager's response is too enthusiastic, and if it refers directly to the quality of the plan or proposal, the intended support can turn a individual's commitment into a kind of imposed assignment: a manager can "take over" the commitment from the employee.

Judgments are most damaging, of course, when they are negative. When responding to people's expressions of commitment, it is essential to focus on the *making* of the commitment, to give positive support to the commitment, and to leave the responsibility and effort to the individual. Consider some examples:

Customer service rep:		I have a great idea to enhance customer service. I will....
Manager:	X	No, that won't work. What I would do is....
	√	Excellent—customer service is crucial. What else have you thought about doing?
Manager:		When can you have that report completed?
Employee:		I can have it on your desk by 9:00 tomorrow morning.
Manager:	X	Be reasonable. You'll never make that deadline.
	√	I look forward to reading it.

The quality of the plan being committed to may seem too low or less than adequate by your standards, but what matters most is whether or not it involves a commitment to a specific behavior. The quality of the plan or the proposed level of activity is not as critical as the making and keeping of a commitment. Your responses must reinforce the commitment *and* the habit of making commitments, especially when an employee is making a commitment to a new activity or behavior. (An effective coach will, however, have a method or process that can be used to help the employee consider the quality of the plan. By asking a few questions, the manager may be able to facilitate additional thinking or another creative approach to the situation.)

Coaching Commitments

While every commitment must be reinforced *as a commitment,* some commitments will always be better than others. If you withhold your judgment on the quality of employees' commitments, how can you have your employees consistently do the things that will make them perform well and get good results?

Gaining the commitments is a crucial first step. Coaching can't really start until commitments are made and kept.

STEP ONE - GAINING COMMITMENT

DO THE PEOPLE **DO** WHAT THEY SAY THEY ARE GOING TO DO?

IF **YES**

IF **NO**

STEP TWO - COACHING

NOTHING TO COACH

INCREASE THE LEVEL OR QUALITY OF COMMITMENT

Figure 9.5
Two-Step Process

Once you have gained commitments, you can begin to *coach* those commitments by setting the expectations up front. With new employees, for instance, job training sets out the steps and the processes. As part of this training, the coach must demonstrate, in real-world situations, the key behaviors and activities—the essentials. Having shown their effectiveness, the coach can then ask the employee to make a commitment to them. If the company makes specific requirements, such as for hours of work, call quotas, reporting procedures, and so on, these need to be agreed upon and committed to from the very outset. In an organization that allows more self-management, however, the manager can ask the new employee to identify and commit to key behaviors and processes. For instance, the employee might be asked to set his or her own result goals, working hours, call commitments, or other activity commitments.

This approach can be highly advantageous, because the more involved an employee is in setting the activity commitments, the more likely it is that he or she will keep those commitments, and the easier it is for the coach to hold the employee accountable. The way to do this is one of the central lessons in all management: establishing an "admission ticket."

The Admission Ticket

The "admission ticket" is one of the most powerful and effective concepts we have brought to managers in North America. It is a critical step in developing a self-management system that will encourage your people to be responsible, accountable self-managers.

As a professional manager, you have invested time, money, effort, and energy into making yourself who and what you are. You have developed your knowledge and skills and acquired experience and expertise. As a result, your time is *valuable*—but how valuable? What is your time worth? What price is put on your time? In other words, what is the perceived value of your time? Of course, the two key perceptions of interest are, first, your own and, second, that of your employees and associates.

To understand better what we mean, consider the relationship between price and value. You will likely agree that people who pay for something always value it more highly than those who do not pay. And the more they pay, the more value they attribute to it. This is a law of human nature—the more we have a commitment to something, the more we tend to value it. For example, if you are someone who bought your first car by saving up earnings from part-time jobs you held while going to school, you know how much you treasured that car and how well you cared for it.

What effective coaches realize is that people who *pay* make a commitment—and the more they pay, the greater their commitment. Consider the following questions—managers' typical answers are quite revealing:

> "Say you're a sales manager. What would your coaching time with a sales rep be like if you could charge them a consulting fee of $500 a day? Would the rep want to start early?"

Managers are usually a bit surprised at the idea, but almost without exception, they answer, "Yes, absolutely!" The dialogue usually continues as follows:

> "Would the rep be fully prepared for a good day's work?"
> "Sure would."
> "Would your rep take long coffee breaks and a leisurely lunch?"
> "Not likely!"
> "Would he or she put in a full day?"
> "Yes indeed."

What does this all suggest? Simply, that if you value your time, you have to set a price on it. If you make it appear that the time you spend with your people is "free" (and inexhaustible), they will perceive the value of your time as low.

To see a professional perform, whether in sports, music, theatre, or any specialized activity, requires an "admission ticket" from every person who wants to enjoy, benefit, or profit from his or her talents or skills. And the higher the price, the higher the expectations for the performance itself. To see the performance, you must buy a ticket—there is a price to pay. In fact, if you show up at the game or event without a ticket, you know you're not getting in. And everyone accepts this as fair. So why shouldn't your people pay to receive the advantages of your time and coaching? You are a professional too. You've earned, and continue to earn, the right.

So what is the admission ticket for your time and coaching expertise? Professionals demand—and get—a high price. Amateurs get no price. Which are you? A professional, of course, but…. You're probably not in a position to charge $500 an day— or any amount of actual money. So, what *can* you charge?

The answer is *effort*. Effort is the admission ticket your people must have to gain your valuable coaching and consulting time. They can all afford that price. But the most effective managers don't simply expect—or demand—that their employees "try hard," or "make an effort," or "do a good job." Those are abstract, generalized demands—the sort of thing that is used in coaxing, not in coaching. Instead, you must identify specific activities that you have trained, and to which your people have made specific commitments. When they fail to keep those commitments (no matter how small), they haven't paid the price of admission.

As Figure 9.6 indicates, you will find your admission tickets among the controllables—among a range of specific, practical, well-defined activities that are essential to good performance. The admission ticket might be based on a number of calls, a weekly caseload, or any commitment the effort eagle has made.

No matter what activity is chosen, setting the admission ticket is proactive: it is something that has to be done, not in response to old results and what has already happened, but so as to begin a new initiative. The admission ticket must also be "excuse-proof." That is, in setting the ticket, you need to consider the time and energy your employees have to spend in reacting to the uncontrollables, and make sure that uncontrollables do not rule out the activity you have identified. With a well-chosen ticket, there can be no excuses—short of a catastrophe—for failing to make the required effort.

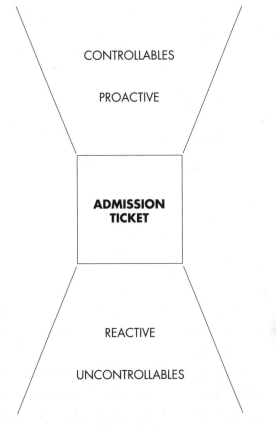

Figure 9.6
Setting Admission Tickets

Allocating Time and Energy

So effort is the admission ticket. A kept commitment is an admission ticket. It's as simple as that—and yet powerfully effective.

Coaching occurs when an admission ticket merits your time and effort; the failure to produce an admission ticket merits no managerial response. When employees fail to keep their effort commitments, managers risk burn-out by coaxing, cajoling, and attempting to motivate from the outside. The experienced coach, however, saves time and energy by refusing to invest: no admission ticket, no reinforcement, no coaching, and especially no coaxing. Management time devoted to "no-ticket" employees is, generally speaking, a poor investment with strictly limited returns. That's an easy ROE decision. On the other hand, anyone who does exhibit effort or satisfactory success habits deserves your best performance: they have paid the price, and it is your professional responsibility to deliver. When employees follow through on the courses of action to which they have committed themselves, it is time for coaches to keep *their own* commitment to coach for skill and effectiveness.

Failing to require and expect an admission ticket dramatically reduces the perceived value of your time, both in your own eyes and the eyes of your employees. When you provide your time "for free," giving it away to anyone who asks for it, and even to people who don't ask for it but are just there, you are saying, in effect, "You don't need to do your part or even work hard, but I'll do my part—training, retraining, coaxing, and worrying about you." You are creating an environment in which there are no expectations and where commitments need not be kept. Where there are "no consequences," you will find yourself, in effect, *reinforcing* a failure to keep commitments.

Requiring an admission ticket sets a fair and reasonable price on your time and effort. It also allows you to reinforce effort as well as results and to begin to use positive reinforcements in preference to negative reinforcements. Those who do carry out the activities that have been identified as essentials will get your attention. And the low-effort employees (those who do not demonstrate the required behavior or keep their commitments) will not. It's as simple as that, but it may save your management career!

This is a critical point in implementing the managing effort system. You may be glad to reduce your use of negative reinforcement; few managers really enjoy punishing their employees or calling people up on the carpet. But you may feel that if you are not making a clear *response* to poor performance, you are not doing anything about the problem. At this point, remember the distinction between telling and showing. When you systematically withdraw coaching time and resources from low-effort employees, and systematically devote your time and resources to people who are making an effort, you are sending a very clear signal. These coaching activities send a far stronger message to both the poor and the satisfactory performers than any amount of telling ever could. Of course, at times, it will be necessary to tell a poor performer what he or she failed to do. But, interestingly, people will see soon enough where your attention is going and figure out what they have to do to earn your time and resources.

A good illustration of the admission ticket's effectiveness was provided by a successful sales manager with a multinational pharmaceutical company. The manager (we'll call him Don) recalled his earlier days as a pharmaceutical rep: his district manager was in town, and he was driving him out for a day of working together. Early in the day, however, the district manager told him to pull the car over and said, "Don, it's apparent to me that you're not managing this day the way you outlined and committed to. Please drop me back at my car, and call me when you're ready to do the job the way you were trained."

"That was the quietest drive I ever had," Don recalled. "I was more than a little concerned about my future with the company. But I learned an important lesson. My manager expected me to keep my commitments, and from then on, that is what I did, whether he was with me or not."

Benefits of the Admission Ticket

As you consider making the "admission ticket" part of your management system, think of its main benefits:

1. The admission ticket approach encourages self-management from the very beginning. As a managerial strategy, it is *firm but fair.* The admission ticket approach lets people know about your coaching system and how to work best with you. It sets the expectation.

2. It is an effective guilt- and stress-*reducer* for the manager, while it is an effective guilt- and stress-*producer* for the low-effort employee. How often have you found yourself feeling guilt or stress over employees who are just not doing the job? The admission ticket approach allows you to say that if they are not doing the job, not making the full effort, it is not your responsibility: it's not your fault if they fail.

3. Asking for an admission ticket saves time and maximizes ROE. The manager saves time because the employees do their part. You don't have to coax them to do it—you coach for skill. Since employees have done their part, your coaching and consulting have a higher return.

4. It encourages team-building, since everyone is managed in the same way, with the same approach. Everyone knows the system, and if you decide to pull time or resources

from one person to devote them elsewhere, everyone understands why.

5. The approach increases coaching opportunities. You can assess the tickets to know where you need to be spending time; accordingly, those who are prepared to benefit get most of the help.

6. The admission ticket works at a practical level *every day:* the essentials you are monitoring can be tracked daily. You don't need to wait until the end of the week, the month, or the quarter. Performance evaluations based on the essentials are always possible and always in order.

7. The strategy is simple and systematic—and because it is systematic, it is predictive. It extends the range of your controllables.

This innovative approach demonstrates in a practical way the ultimate working relationship between manager and employee: "You do your part, and I'll do my part." It unequivocally sets the expectation that employees will take responsibility for that which is theirs—the making and keeping of commitments. (And we have discussed earlier the impressive power of such expectations.) An admission ticket policy establishes the most vital of all expectations. We sum it up as follows:

• The employee has commitments.
• The employee keeps those commitments.
• Now the manager has commitments.

In short, the admission ticket is central to an effective management system.

If this all makes sense to you, as it we know it has to many successful leaders, then you need to think about

• establishing the admission ticket—the essential efforts and behaviors you expect employees to make consistently

during their employment with you
- expecting the admission ticket
- requiring the admission ticket—holding your people responsible and accountable
- reinforcing effort and kept commitments

Keep in mind that a dedicated manager does not use the admission ticket to avoid working with people. In fact, the approach challenges the manager to spend a considerable amount of time thinking about how to help the people who are putting in an effort. It also allows the manager to support people who are making an effort by providing the highest possible levels of coaching and consulting. People who have the admission ticket—the desired performance—deserve your best performance in return. When you, as a manager, keep your end of the bargain, the admission ticket approach will have long-term benefits.

The approach is basically fair-minded. When specific activities are the admission ticket for your time and support, it is always just the *facts* that determine whether or not a person gets your reinforcement. Success (and failure) will not depend on personality or character (neither of which can be changed, in any event) but rather on effort (entirely controllable) and results (in a self-management system, increasingly controllable). The approach is also fair because it makes for *consistency,* and it doesn't depend on passing circumstances. Your people will have the sense that there are steady, reliable criteria for performance, and this will counteract the rollercoaster effect of allotting coaching time and resources based on results achieved or on some formula of "equal time for all." Admission tickets provide a set of constant expectations, no matter how the results look: work doesn't stop just because a quota is met, only to be kickstarted in a panicky attempt to meet the next objective. And your people can be successful *every* day, rather than having to wait for an all-or-nothing judgment based on periodic results.

When you require an admission ticket, you make it easy to manage your own effort effectively. There's no need for lectures or "parent-child" relationships. Instead, you devote your time to supporting the people who are making the effort. And in this way, of course, you conserve energy, save time, and increase ROE—both your employees' and your own.

REINFORCE THE ESSENTIALS

AND FACILITATE

SELF-REINFORCEMENT.

Chapter Ten

CREATING A SELF-MANAGEMENT SYSTEM: STEP THREE

Standard Procedures

As you consciously and systematically develop an environment for coaching and self-management by identifying the essentials and making them the admission ticket for your time, your associates will soon realize how and where your attention is directed. They will begin to see you as a coach with a defined, systematic approach to management, and, together, you can all begin to contribute to an environment oriented towards effort, performance, and improved results. But what must you be doing, every day, to coach effectively? You have begun to allocate your time and effort differently, but what exactly do you do with it, on a day-to-day basis? You need *daily* coaching procedures, guided by a coaching system, to reinforce and support effort, as well as results.

It is easy and important to reinforce results: we always do, conditioned as we are by our upbringing, education, and work experience. The world seems to recognize results, whether good or bad. This apparently "natural" response cannot be neglected; we must continue to systematically reinforce results. However, it may be necessary to develop better habits for reinforcing *effort.* "Trying hard" is commonly regarded as the *second-best* thing people can do—after *winning.* Effort is typically considered only when the results are disappointing.

This conventional attitude must be adjusted. Insofar as you are a "manager," effort is *all* that you can "manage" in yourself and all that you can coach in others. While results will always count for a great deal, a coach must also focus on the components of *performance,* for it is in that area that major differences can be made, differences that will achieve better results.

Reinforcement Options

Good coaching is primarily a matter of doing what you have always done, but more consciously and more frequently. When you coach, you use reinforcement and feedback deliberately and effectively, not just because it seems a "natural" response. And you use it not only to support people who are committing themselves to, and performing, the essentials but to help them reinforce *themselves.* As long as it is up to you to identify the behaviors and attitudes associated with good performance in your workplace, and to approve the people who exhibit them consistently, you will find it hard to break out of the "motivational" model that limits—and exhausts—many managers. Those essentials must become habits, and *habits* can only be formed by individuals. But the coach can help, by encouraging individuals to express, and take responsibility for, their own reinforcement.

We have already discussed reinforcement theory and its relationship to motivation. At the outset, the coach's choices are fairly straightforward. Look at your people's effort—their actual behaviors and attitudes—and decide what you want to see in the future.

Effective coaches systematically reinforce, train, and support the attitudes and constructive behaviors they want to reoccur. As much as 90% of the coach's activity may be focused on *positively* reinforcing desirable attitudes and behaviors. An important, but carefully restricted, amount of time and effort (perhaps as little as 10%) may be directed towards "neutral" non-reinforcement (a simple withdrawal of attention) and explicitly *negative* reinforcement of undesirable attitudes and behaviors. On a day-to-day basis, the manager has these three options, and each can take a variety of specific forms.

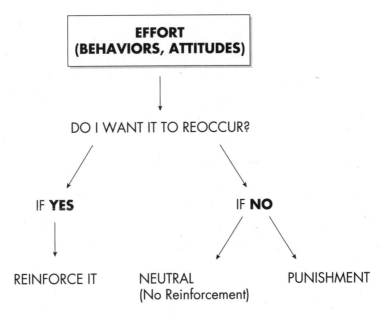

Figure 10.1
Day-to-Day Decisioning

However, there are many more ways to supply positive reinforcement. Directing as little as 10% of your activity to neutral and negative reinforcement is not just a good coaching strategy—it's a practical necessity. There simply aren't very many ways in which a manager can apply effective *negative* reinforcement.

Reinforcement Objectives

In their day-to-day activities, coaches concentrate on training and supporting specific attitudes and actions. The focus is always on the *observable:* not on what you may expect of a person, not on your "reading" of his or her mind, but on what you can see of his or her performance. A coach is always on the lookout for occasions to provide positive reinforcement, but it is essential to reward observed, objective actions and results, rather than inferred, internal attributes or characteristics.

This approach relies strictly on observation. It deals with the external attitudes and actions that you can see plainly, and it makes no attempt to get "inside" a person's individual psychology. Sometimes this approach requires a special effort. We often allow our perceptions of *how* people behave to be colored by speculations about *why* they behave as they do. Effective coaching does not require any special insight *into* people, just clear, objective observations of what they do. Only in this way is it possible to deal correctly with questions of motivations, which remain private and internal. There are two ways to get at those motivations. The first is simply to observe behavior and attitudes—these are the best, and in some cases, the only, external evidence of motivation. By attending to behavior and attitudes, an empathetic coach can often identify a person's basic drives and deepest interests. The second method is to ask—and to listen carefully. Where there is an atmosphere of trust, people's descriptions of their motivations, ambitions, and goals can be made the foundation of effective reinforcement and self-development. However, people may not be entirely honest about themselves, especially if they feel they are expected to say certain things or profess certain goals. A thoughtful listener can take account of this effect and hear the genuine self-expression behind an easy or a conventional answer. It is crucial to respond to that expression and to make it clear that when you ask a question, you depend on an honest answer.

Reprimands

As we have noted, effective coaching limits the use of punishments: only in this way can negative reinforcement have a significant impact. Too much negative reinforcement (fines, penalties, withdrawal of privileges, and scolding) will appear as nothing more than the actions of a dictator. Dictators can coerce a certain amount of behavior, but they do not win respect or commitment.

However, when an immediate, direct response to unproductive or destructive attitudes and behaviors is necessary, negative reinforcement can extinguish undesirable behaviors. Non-reinforcement or a withdrawal of attention may not work quickly enough. Neutral non-reinforcement is preferable, but when a workplace issue must be resolved quickly, merely withholding reinforcement may not be practical. For instance, if someone commits a gross violation of standard practices—steals, forges a signature, or misrepresents a product to customers—a direct negative response is demanded.

Sometimes, then, a negative reinforcement will be required. To have maximum effect, however, reprimands must be used rarely. As we have suggested, the ideal coaching mix is 90% positive reinforcement and 10% negative reinforcement; in the same way, the best mix of the 10% negative reinforcement is 9% neutral non-reinforcement and 1% punishment. The significant contrast between positive and negative reinforcement gives the latter its point and emphasis. Compare the hockey coach who yells at his players just *once* a season to the coach who never stops yelling. Whose reprimands are likely to be more effective?

Effective coaching reprimands are short and sharp, and bear strictly on a problematic activity or performance. They are framed as *reports,* not judgments; they refer to observable actions, not the character of the person who is responsible for the actions. Reprimands make a specific point and imply no general conclusion. They leave (or show) a way to move on:

"That complaint should have been handled at once."

NOT "You do not deal with people very well."

"*That* was a bad decision."

NOT "You have bad judgment."

"This proposal needs some rethinking—and some rewriting."

NOT "You do not understand the market, and you

obviously didn't think this through."

Support and Non-support

A distinction between support and non-support may be helpful in developing (or re-evaluating) your reinforcement strategies. The two terms offer a flexible way of analyzing what you do to reinforce others, where you direct these reinforcements, and what effect they have.

Managers tend to be naturally supportive or non-supportive. The naturally *supportive* manager tends to be *supportive* of good efforts and supportive of poor efforts. The naturally *non-supportive* manager tends to be *non-supportive* of poor efforts and *non-supportive* of good efforts. So, is it best to be supportive or non-supportive? Yes! It depends on what you are supporting—or not.

When analyzing whether you are naturally "supportive" or "non-supportive," you may have to reconsider the way you usually distinguish between positive and negative reinforcement. "Support" includes, of course, rewards for good results, but it also refers to a wide range of responses and actions that your people perceive, consciously or unconsciously, as approving, validating, or at least *condoning* their behavior.

Even responses that are framed and intended as negative reinforcements may be *received* as a kind of support. For example, employees may accept, even welcome, a scolding for poor performance or bad results, feeling that in this way they are "paying" for their failure and that they will then be able to leave it behind them.

The support/non-support distinction helps to identify various possible allocations of managerial energy—different managerial "styles." One of the most important distributions to recognize (and to change!) is typical of well-meaning managers who possess a natural supportiveness without a proper sense of where to direct it.

EFFORT

	HIGH	LOW
SUPPORT	COACH	COAX
NON-SUPPORT	DESTRUCTIVE	COACH

Figure 10.2
Managerial Style: Coaxing

These managers risk burn-out (and depress overall perform-ance levels) by devoting time and energy to the "wrong" people (those who are not demonstrating good attitudes, making the effort, and/or getting the results). Such an allocation of energy is characteristic of the "coax." Time and effort are squandered in an impractical attempt to change people's effort levels. A typical example would be the manager who supports non-effort by listening to an employee's excuses for not keeping a commitment, then gives energy to the excuses by disputing or even discussing them, and finally offers a pep-talk, encouraging the employee to keep the commitment next time.

A well-developed coaching system would be diagrammed as follows:

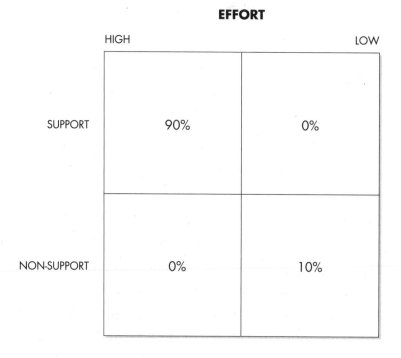

EFFORT

	HIGH	LOW
SUPPORT	90%	0%
NON-SUPPORT	0%	10%

Figure 10.3
Ideal System

No energy at all ought to be used to support non-effort, and only the minimum of energy is required to punish non-effort. The coach's main focus is on supporting effort.

The choice, finally, is not between being supportive or non-supportive. You must be both—that is, you must be supportive, but only of the *right things*. Naturally supportive managers are typically empathetic; they can see things from other people's point of view. They may also, however, identify too deeply and personally with an employee and his or her point of view, losing sight of the larger context and the proper roles of the coach and manager. Empathy, which allows the coach to observe and support positive behaviors and attitudes, may be replaced by *sympathy*, an unconditional support for the person, regardless of his or her specific actions or circumstances. Naturally supportive managers, while they are likely to do a good job of supporting effort, may have to learn not to support non-effort.

Other managers may be appropriately not supporting non-effort, spending little time and energy on people who don't work. These managers, however, may also need to learn how to do a better job of supporting effort. The time they save by refusing to get involved in performance problems and effort issues ought to be directed towards good performers and opportunities for growth.

Some of the time, being supportive is the correct coaching strategy, and some of the time, being non-supportive is the correct strategy. A naturally supportive manager needs to effectively reduce support for low- or no-effort performers, while a naturally non-supportive manager needs to effectively increase support for high-effort performers.

Promoting Self-Reinforcement

Day-to-day reinforcement and support procedures have a long-term goal, which is to move the process to a higher level. Your objective, finally, is to have employees *internalize* a reinforcement structure for effort and support that you have helped create. It is essential to develop self-managing, self-reinforcing employees, since in today's work environment, most work is done without direct supervision. Reinforcement theory shows that a positive reinforcement is most effective if it occurs very soon after the behavior. Unsupervised work, then, often cannot be effectively supported by a manager; the reinforcements are likely to come "too late," and their application may be misunderstood. Telling an employee on Friday afternoon that he or she "had a great week," for example, is rather general and may be less effective than discussing the specific behaviors you really intend to reinforce.

Therefore, employees must learn to *reinforce themselves*. The role of the coach is to help develop and mold the employee's own self-reinforcement structure. This structure must be constructed and maintained "from the inside out." Unless it is informed by the *individual's* interests and abilities, it cannot become a structure of *self*-reinforcement.

As is usually the case when taking a coaching approach, asking, not telling, is the key. If you begin by simply handing out approval—telling them they did well—your people will register and enjoy your support. And then they will wait for more of the same. Instead, you need to begin to transfer the work of reinforcement by asking them the right questions, at the right time, about the things they did well. Good coaching, instead of generalizing ("Way-to-go!"), invites achievers to evaluate or congratulate themselves:

"What did you do well?"

"How do you feel about it?"

Such an exercise is possible at any time. These questions develop conscious competence. Achievers can talk about current circumstances or relive past successes. When people begin to appreciate, for themselves, the efforts they have made, they will begin to provide their own internal reinforcement. They will also associate the effort and the results with external rewards. These external reinforcements must follow the internal sense of achievement and accomplishment.

It's never too early to start developing internal reinforcements, as the following true story suggests. Buster, a four-year-old, comes off the ice after skating lessons. His mother is there watching. "How did I do?" asked Buster, looking up. "How do you think you did?" his mother asked. A big smile, and then, "I think I did great!" Four years old, and already self-reinforcing!

Improving Reinforcement Systems

More specific coaching questions can help tie self-reinforcements to particular effort habits:

- What do you feel went well?
- How did you reward yourself for that good result?

The more people discuss their successes and the steps, the process, or the efforts that produced them, the more effective their self-reinforcement, and the more likely they are to repeat the behaviors.

This kind of discussion can be supported until, in the long run, the employee becomes effectively self-reinforcing. Ideally, the coach provides only 5–10% of an employee's support, and most of that is used to sustain the individual's *self*-management. The coach becomes the indirect, qualitative manager. Any positive reinforcement that he or she provides is, finally, an "add-on":

Coach: How do you feel about your presentation?

Employee: I think it went well—I'm getting better at it.

Coach: What exactly made it go well?

Employee: I did some extra work on the figures, and I tried to anticipate the audience's specific concerns.

Coach: How do you know that created the desired response?

Employee: I felt they took me more seriously. A couple of people stayed behind to ask for my advice about some of the points I raised. I thought that I did a good job.

Coach: I think so too.

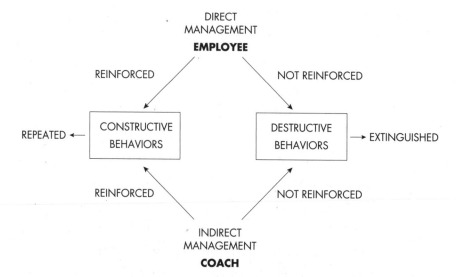

Figure 10.4
Ideal Reinforcement System

Feedback

Self-reinforcement is developed by means of effective feedback. Feedback by itself is not necessarily reinforcement; it can be merely information.

However, when feedback is interpreted by the receiver and when it has an impact, it becomes reinforcement. Feedback, whether it has a positive, neutral, or negative effect, depends on five factors:

1. The timing of response: when is feedback required?
2. The frequency of response: how often is feedback required?
3. The consistency of response: are timing, frequency, and occasion predictably associated?
4. The type of response: what form (oral/written, informal/formal, etc.) and tone (positive/negative) will it take?
5. The impact of response: what behavior or attitude is it intended to reinforce?

Faulty Feedback Models

It is important to avoid a number of common, but faulty, feedback models. Feedback can become confusing and, therefore, ineffective when any of the factors listed above are not carefully integrated in a systematic, reliable program of response and reinforcement. Sometimes the fault has to do with *timing*. For instance, failing to respond to effort, even before long-term results are in, is one of the most serious and common mistakes a manager can make. From the employees' point of view, it is seldom true that "no news is good news." If they are getting no feedback on their efforts, they *may* assume that they are underperforming, and they *may* try harder. But they may also decide that their effort is simply not being noticed, since you are not reinforcing it. From a manager's point of view, it is often a mistake to "leave well enough alone."

Feedback may also be faulty because it fails to discriminate carefully between occasions for response. This is very common when managers look exclusively at results, not at the effort that produced the performance.

The indiscriminate "Way-to-go!", usually based on results, has a confusing effect, as it fails to discriminate between varying levels of performance and effort. Blanket approval may in fact provide inappropriate support for poor effort, and insufficient support for excellent effort. Managers must, indeed, congratulate both results and performance, and they must also provide varying levels of reinforcement for varying levels of performance. For example, by recognizing and evaluating the level of effort *in the process,* as well as the end result that the series of initiatives produces, the manager can provide specific feedback on the real determinants of performance and success.

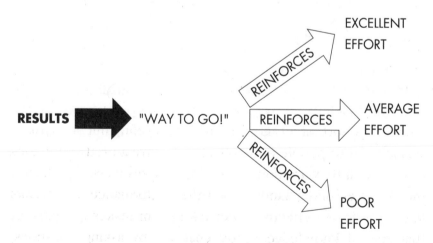

Figure 10.5
Confused Feedback Model

Confusion may also stem from choosing the wrong form of behavior and response. The best example, already discussed in other contexts, is responding to non-effort by coaxing. Non-effort may indeed be an occasion for feedback, but what is usually required is *non*-reinforcement or, if the lack of effort is flagrant, a quick, efficient reprimand. There is no point in trying to turn non-performance into a learning opportunity—what has to be learned is that effort is required.

Ideal Feedback System

Faulty feedback models are usually unidirectional: "feedback" is too narrowly understood as an exercise in which the manager is the *active* participant and the employee is a *passive* recipient. To get the most out of typical feedback situations, such as weekly development meetings, impromptu discussions, and annual performance appraisals, a good coach establishes a communication loop. It is just as important to *ask* employees about performance factors as it is to *tell* them about the results and the consequences. Having asked, it is essential to *listen:* the most valuable feedback a coach can provide has to do with a person's plans and needs, as well as their results up to that moment.

However, feedback, especially in formal situations, is often regarded as a kind of "report card" on the employee's performance. This sort of evaluation may be useful, but it is easily available. Your people probably already have a pretty good idea of how well they are doing, and, in some respects, they have a much better understanding of their performance and results than you do. An effective feedback system makes the most of that special knowledge. Good coaches, by asking questions, encourage internal feedback strategies that become *self*-evaluation and *self*-reinforcement. This approach helps employees develop an *internal* feedback process that parallels the external process and which is, in the long run, more powerful and productive.

In the ideal feedback system, the manager and employee both reinforce constructive behaviors. Destructive behaviors are, on the manager's side, "ignored": they are not reinforced, not supported, not made the focus of any redemptive scheme. On the employees' side, destructive behaviors are also not reinforced (by complaints, "confessions," or excuses). Where there are no accusations, no excuses are required: employees do not have to dwell on failure or make any grandiose promises to change or to reform themselves. Instead, the alignment of the internal and external processes develops confidence and encourages the raising of expectations.

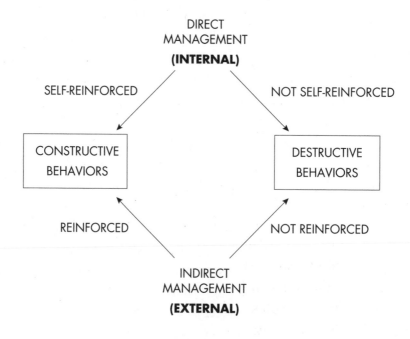

Figure 10.6
Ideal Feedback System

A key coaching objective, then, is to use every feedback situation to help people identify their strengths and opportunities for growth. This often involves *asking*. "Returning the question" is the best response to those who ask, "How am I doing?" or "What should I do?" The people asking those questions already know the answers; they may only need the opportunity, and the encouragement, to work it out for themselves.

Some independent-thinking sales managers in the pharmaceutical industry have applied these feedback strategies by having their sales reps submit a plan for the training time they will spend with their district managers. The plan must be handed in well before the actual training day and must include a schedule or agenda, training or learning objectives, etc. After the training session, the rep submits a report discussing what he or she felt was accomplished and what areas require following up—the sort of performance review that in many systems is carried out by the manager. The managers who use this method are often amazed at how well—and how productively—their sales reps respond when they are made responsible for their own business and career development. But the results aren't really surprising. This approach—an excellent illustration of the managing effort system—benefits from the enlarged potential that is created by *asking* rather than telling, and thereby giving ownership of and responsibility for the business to the person who needs to own it and be responsible for it.

THE MORE YOU PROACT,

THE LESS YOU WILL HAVE TO REACT.

Chapter Eleven

SYSTEMATIC COACHING

Coaching Strategies

A good coaching system involves the use of strategies that identify, but do not support, poor performance and that ensure good performers get the recognition and reinforcement they deserve. These strategies vary according to each employee's place in the effort grid: the coach reinforces effort and results, so the more effort and results, the more the coach has to do.

Golden Eagles

Coaching Self-Managers

Golden eagles are a coach's first priority. They are already making an effort, performing well, and getting good results. They have the most impact and offer the most potential. Congratulations are in order, but that is only the beginning. Managers sometimes go so far as to avoid golden eagles, thinking that they don't need coaching. Golden eagles indeed require the least amount of *basic* coaching. After all, they have good abilities and strongly developed self-managing and self-reinforcing skills, and they typically have good work habits. They require a certain amount of maintenance, but *growth* is more important. They need challenges and coaching on development. The question is not really the *amount* of coaching but the *kind* of coaching you provide. Your best performers deserve your own best performance, qualitatively as well as quantitatively. They offer the most to reinforce, both in terms of results and efforts. You must reinforce and reward both, but keep in mind two priorities: conscious competence and continuous growth. Golden eagles will naturally enjoy your expressions of appreciation, but remember that they are more deeply and genuinely motivated by an inner sense of ambition and achievement. Your best strategy, then, is to build conscious competence, to get them to reflect on their strengths and to identify growth areas. In this way, you can help them set higher expectations, redefine goals, and identify new *challenges.* Your coaching must continue to encourage their self-management and recognize their ability to move ahead. The relationship with golden eagles often becomes a partnership. The time you spend with them has little or nothing to do with supervising, directing, or any form of top-down management, leaving both partners free to look ahead to shared long-term objectives and new possibilities. If anything, it is a consultative approach to coaching.

Systematic Coaching for Golden Eagles

A management *system* is based on *scheduled* coaching. On a day-to-day basis, it is important to deal with a variety of short-term goals, practical necessities, and long-term objectives. But the more time you spend *reacting* to issues, the less time you will have for effective coaching. A scheduled approach, typically centered on a weekly development interview (WDI), will ensure both the adequacy and consistency of your coaching. And the more you accomplish *proactively* through good coaching and development, the less there will be to *react* to each day. A scheduled approach will not only ensure that you spend time with your golden eagles but will also create a proactive agenda for the meeting.

Systematic coaching consists primarily in scheduling regular, one-on-one coaching and development time. In addition, take every opportunity to reinforce good results and strong efforts. Scheduled coaching sessions, however, will provide the backbone of your system. Sessions of this nature are designed to have the employee carry out four critical activities:

1. Review performance, commitments, and results;
2. Review goals and commitments for the future;
3. Consult on tactics and strategy; and
4. Identify the required resources.

These components are essential whether you are coaching a golden eagle or a talent trap. In every individual case, however, the basic activities will be determined by the employee, with the coach acting as consultant.

Golden Eagle: Review

The coaching questions that begin a golden eagle's coaching meeting are designed to check the good performer's self-reinforcing structure and to encourage self-reinforcement. Questions must reflect the self-confidence model and its "90% strengths, 10% growth opportunities" allocation as shown in Figure 11.1.

This model provides a solid foundation for every coaching activity. Using the same pattern will condition the employee to approach his or her situation in the same confident manner. The review questions begin with the positives, and then move on to consider growth areas:

- How was your week (month, year)?
- What went well?
- What did you learn?
- Is there anything you would change?

In reviewing a golden eagle's activities and results, you want them to talk about their successes, their accomplishments, and their efforts. Your object is to provide an opportunity for self-evaluation and self-reinforcement, and to corroborate that self-reinforcement. With golden eagles, this is usually easy: efforts and results are usually positive. Most good performers have strong self-management skills and will tend to concentrate on the controllable aspects of their performance without any special prompting. Golden eagles can be encouraged to review their results: these results are typically good and are easy to reinforce. And because golden eagles are interested in getting more good results, they are naturally inclined to examine the process and be aware of the efforts that went into achieving them.

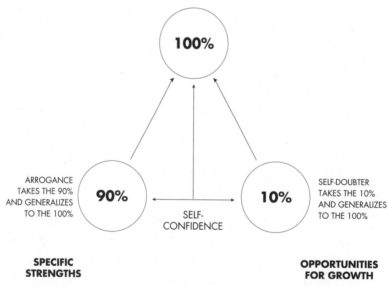

Figure 11.1
Self-Confidence Model

The review needs to focus on actual cases and situations. In this way, specific coaching opportunities will make themselves apparent. Let the process take its course. Let golden eagles tell you when and where they need help. If necessary, make a note, but wait until later to follow up with suggestions or recommendations. Taking the time to listen, and in this way acknowledging efforts and successes, is a powerful way to reinforce employees and their behavior. Also, when employees are telling you about their efforts and results, they are also *telling themselves*. This is a critical part of self-reinforcement and an important component of self-management in general. The coach provides the add-ons, reinforcing the reinforcer.

The review lets golden eagles clarify their successes and reinforce themselves. At the same time, it sets the agenda for the rest of the coaching session. When the employee is feeling positive, it is time for the second component.

Golden Eagles: Goals and Commitments

Coaching questions for the second part of the coaching session capitalize on the positive feelings and conscious competence developed in the review of activities and results:

- What are your goals for the next week?
- What are the key commitments you will make to achieve the goals?
- What growth areas or opportunities for development will you target next?

These questions encourage golden eagles to challenge themselves, to "raise the bar" for their performance and set new goals. Since they have a good sense of their strengths, golden eagles usually come up with well-formed and worthwhile challenges for themselves. The specific quantity or quality of the commitment, however, is not the main issue. The coaching questions and the answers are not meant to establish a quota or a performance standard, but to sustain and encourage a good performer's habit of resetting expectations and making commitments. Rather than judge the commitments your golden eagles are ready to make, ask questions, to help them formulate specific commitments, and consult freely on goals, plans, and strategies:

- How will you do that?
- How will you carry out the process, or what will you add to it?

When goals and commitments have become sufficiently clear, the third component of the coaching session can be effectively introduced.

Golden Eagles: Resources

In coaching for commitment, the emphasis is always on the one person who can follow through: the employee. Once those commitments are established, however, the coach can make his or her own contribution. Coaching questions at this point of the session can usefully address specific needs:

- What do you require?
- Do you anticipate any other needs?
- What help do you need from me?

As a coach, your own experience and advice are most appropriate in connection with the specific commitments that your golden eagles make for themselves. Now is the time to return to any earlier comments that suggested training needs or extra resources and to offer recommendations.

Take care, however, that such contributions, even though they are made very carefully, do not create any dependence. Every so often, ask resource questions that clearly indicate *who* is responsible for the performer's growth:

- What are you working on for self-development?
- What skills/knowledge/personal abilities are you working on?

Growth is a key source of satisfaction for golden eagles and, therefore, an important part of any employer's strategies to engage employees on a personal basis and to retain employees for the organization. Good performers who feel that they are constantly developing, moving from strength to strength, will be less interested in changing companies or managers. Golden eagles who do not feel that they are growing will soon look for opportunities elsewhere.

Wind up the session by scheduling the next one. The effectiveness of this coaching approach depends on continuity, consistency, and a genuine interest in the golden eagles' success. A regular schedule reflects your ongoing commitment to good performers and their development.

Golden Eagles: Consultation

While a formal review process is important, a great deal of the interaction between a golden eagle and his or her manager is spontaneous and unscripted. Golden eagles tend to evaluate their progress and methods of operation on a fairly consistent basis. In talking to managers, they often talk business. They will tend to verbalize their intentions and perceptions, and they will typically invite input from competent, experienced associates—including, ideally, the manager. This informal consultation is, for the manager or coach, one of the most enjoyable aspects of management, and it provides a real sense of satisfaction, accomplishment, and partnership. As much as possible, then, you must attempt to create opportunities for consultation, both on a daily basis and in the formal review sessions.

Effort Eagles

Coaching for Self-Management

When coaching golden eagles, the main goal is to support any self-managing and self-reinforcing skills that are already established and encourage the development of more. With effort eagles, the process is more complex than with golden eagles, since you must reinforce and reward effort and performance, even when there are not necessarily any results. And when you coach effort eagles, much more work must be done simply to put those self-managing skills in place. Most of that work, of course, has to be done by the effort eagle. However, they have paid the price of admission, and that simple achievement must itself be reinforced. Your goal, as a coach, is to help turn that effort into good performance by developing talent and modifying opportunity. Once again, the first priority is to develop conscious competence, to create a sense of achievement and an awareness of possibilities. Given that foundation, the next priority is to encourage growth. And once again, an important tool is the regular, scheduled coaching and training session.

Effort Eagles: Review

In the case of effort eagles, the review of activities that opens the coaching session is often complicated by *results* issues. As we noted above—and as the results grid has shown—golden eagles usually get very good results, so it is easy for them to talk about good results *and* the effort issues on which coaching focuses. Effort eagles, however, only *sometimes* get very good results. When this happens, the coaching session proceeds much as it would with a golden eagle. With effort eagles, as with every group, it is important to reinforce results, whenever the results are there. However, effort eagles are not likely to get *consistently* good results. When results have been poor, they are quite likely to focus on that, to the exclusion of what may have been good effort. They may even be hoping to use the coaching session to "confess" poor results and be "forgiven."

As the effort grid indicates, the focus with effort eagles is on talent: that is the area in which they fall short of golden eagles and may even be surpassed by talent traps. To discuss talent issues, however, may take a few steps. Initial coaching questions can be designed to discover an employee's circumstances and mood:

- How did your week go?
- What went well?
- What did you learn?

Answers to these questions will soon reveal where the effort eagle is focusing. The questions are designed to begin with the positives and to encourage effort eagles to express their feelings about their work. Keep the focus on controllables and effort. Subsequent coaching questions, then, can relate the results— whether good or bad—to growth:

- How did your activity commitments go?
- What went well?
- Where do you need to grow or develop?
- How can you improve?

Questions like these provide an opportunity to recognize the positive aspect of even the poorest results, by opening up the larger sequence of *interim* results:

- What results did you get *in the process?*

Effort eagles need to evaluate their effectiveness in terms of taking control of effort and keeping their commitments, rather than remain fixated on their results. Effective coaching can help employees develop a sense of satisfaction in having made and kept commitments. In short, they will learn to see themselves as *successful.* Even if the desired results are not obtained, they can recognize that they performing up to their potential in the execution phase. Feelings of success are crucial to effective self-reinforcement and, eventually, self-management. Effort eagles must discover—and feel—that there is a return on effort in simply having kept their commitments.

In some cases, a results issue may appear to be intractable. Intervene to put it aside, and get the coaching session back on track. Ask an effort eagle who can't (or won't) concentrate on effort a few direct, practical questions, so as to focus on the aspects of performance, rather than the uncontrollable results:

- Can you see yourself getting better results at your current activity level?
- Can you see yourself getting better results at your current skill level?
- What do you see as needing improvement?

Keep the questions in line with the "90% strengths-10% growth opportunities" model, and focus the discussion on sensible, short-term solutions. In most cases, a problem with results will be related to skill issues. Identify the skills that are needed to improve performance, ask the employee for a self-evaluation in those areas, and schedule a specific training session. In this way, you can acknowledge the effort eagle's sense of disappointment, but balance it with feelings of success, offset it with a constructive plan, and move on to the other important purposes of the coaching session.

Effort Eagles: Goals and Commitments

Coaching questions for effort eagles tend to be the same as those for golden eagles, although there may be slightly more attention paid to the short term. Proceed fairly quickly to the details:

- What is your goal for the next week?
- What are the key commitments you will make to achieve that goal?
- What will your daily schedule look like?

The focus is on coaching the process. This involves getting the employee to identify the stages, set out the controllables, and allocate effort effectively. Effort eagles need to identify commitments that are worthwhile and feasible. Remember that the *making* and *keeping* of commitments are the critical issues in developing self-managing employees. The quality of performance can be worked on over time, but commitment to effort is immediate.

Effort Eagles: Resources

The coaching questions in the last stage of the coaching session are more or less the same as those for golden eagles, but they may lead to more concrete or detailed considerations. Effort eagles may require more direct suggestions, and they usually need training, to develop their skills, as well as coaching, to develop their confidence. It is important, however, to refrain from *telling* effort eagles what they need to do. Managers can usually spot talent issues very easily, and it may be very tempting to *apply* a solution, rather than allow the employee to develop one. Make sure that effort eagles are encouraged to formulate their own needs and to make their own commitments:

- How do you think I can help?
- What resources do you expect from me?

Effort Eagles: Keep the Process Going

At the end of the coaching session, provide a summary. Express your recognition of what they do well; reinforce their good attitudes and strong efforts, but do so in specific terms. A blanket "way to go" will not be convincing or constructive. As a coach, your detailed feedback can provide the *qualitative* reinforcement that the results alone may not have supplied, and, in this way, effort eagles can learn more about their successes and the reinforcements they can provide for themselves. To help them develop and strengthen self-managing and self-reinforcing abilities, make it clear that you are both involved in an ongoing process. End each coaching session by scheduling the next one, and ask them to recap the achievements they expect by that time.

Talent Traps

No Ticket, No Admission

Talent traps pose a complex challenge to coaches. They may be very likeable people. Often it's their personality and interpersonal skills that have brought them to you. From time to time they will turn in a good performance, and sometimes good results. But remember, they get by on talent, not discipline and hard work. While you need to reinforce their results, you must be careful *not* to reinforce their non-effort. The danger is that you will create a faulty feedback situation in which, while you are trying to say, "Your results are good, but your effort levels are low," the talent trap will hear, "Your results are good, mumble mumble," or even, "Your results are good, way to go."

The time you spend coaching talent traps must be related to both their results *and* their effort, and the most effective reinforcement is provided only when they show effort. Otherwise, talent traps can safely be left alone, and their coaching sessions may, indeed, be very short. If they are not making an effort, you must make it clear that they continue to be employed only because of their results.

Talent Traps: Review

Regular coaching sessions are still appropriate for talent traps, who may have some potential. But remember that these are *development* meetings. If the coaching session doesn't offer any real opportunity for building self-managing and self-reinforcing skills, the meeting need not go beyond the review of results. A talent trap who refuses the opportunity to develop only needs a short session, devoted primarily to making specific commitments. If that doesn't happen, the meeting is over.

The opening questions, therefore, are more specific and targeted than the questions you use for a golden eagle or effort eagle. Move as quickly as possible to specific commitment questions:

- How did your new schedule go?
- How did your commitments go?

Talent traps will focus on their results. If the results were good, they will be happy to talk (and talk) about them. If the results were disappointing, they may be ready with circumstantial explanations, intriguing second thoughts, plausible excuses, and compelling rationalizations. Move quickly, then, to questions that refer immediately to the *controllables* and that can only be answered in terms of *effort.*

Such questions will stem the tide of rationales and excuses, and they may persuade talent traps to face specific effort issues that are inhibiting their performance. A talent trap who seems ready to deal with these issues can be encouraged, and the coaching session can immediately proceed to a practical examination of goals and commitments.

Sometimes talent traps will have good results, and they will typically expect congratulations. A coach knows the importance of good results but also realizes that poor effort must never be reinforced. That is why good coaches avoid generalizations such as "You had a good week." That remark might apply only to good results, but a talent trap might very well take it to apply to effort as well. Some managers, to prevent this misinterpretation, are inclined to "moralize." That is, they acknowledge the good results and then go on to infer and praise the efforts that supposedly produced them. But these inferred efforts remain purely hypothetical; no one is really pleased, or fooled, by this sort of displaced reinforcement. Instead, make your position clear by moving *directly* to the goals and commitments phase of the coaching session. This will make it clear to the talent trap that, even though last week's results may have been good, keeping commitments to the effort activities is important.

Talent Traps: Goals and Commitments

Expressing precise goals and objectives, as well as making commitments to specific tasks and activities, is essential for the development of a person who is currently a talent trap. Unfortunately, talent traps are usually not inclined to commit themselves to specific efforts. In fact, they characteristically avoid making commitments to others and especially to themselves. You must make the process short and sweet, even though talent traps will typically have a thousand ways to defer or prolong it. Give them an opportunity to set an admission ticket. If they do, they can be handled as effort eagles or even as golden eagles. When coaching a talent trap, it is critical that the development interview be different when they do pay the price. When they don't, just leave them alone.

Good coaching questions must help the talent trap move quickly from vague, generally acceptable expressions of ambition and "shoulds" to more specific thoughts and statements.

An approach that works well for managers in our client companies is to have talent traps think through their current situation. The manager facilitates their self-assessment of where they are and how they are doing. This sort of facilitating must be viewed as a process, an ongoing series of activities that will help the individual employee develop self-management behaviors. It is not a one-time "selling" job; the manager is not manipulating the employee in any way. In fact, the more the process is turned into a "sale," the less effect it will have, and later, when you try to renew the process, it will have even less effect.

A coaching session with a talent trap may begin with a fairly neutral question, such as

• How do you feel about... ?

The way you complete this question depends on a number of factors, but a common version is as follows:

• How do you feel about the way your year is going so far?

The response of talent traps to such a question is unpredictable, and the degree of their involvement and co-operation will depend on many other considerations, such as the level of trust in your relationship, whether or not they suspect you have an "agenda," and so on. In any case, the key is to encourage the talent traps to talk about how they are feeling and about their career progress.

The next step is to become more specific:

• What would you like to accomplish?

This question addresses goals and objectives. If you have been working in a management role for any length of time, you will know that some people cannot answer this question easily. Good self-managers have conscious, explicit, specific goals, both for the short and the long term. People who cannot talk directly and simply about their goals probably lack self-management skills and typically pose a challenge to the coach. They may have "lofty" goals but are not willing to pay the price. Talent traps, in particular, tend to evade questions about goals and objectives. In some cases, they are proud of their skills and of what they are doing; that is enough for them, and they do not consider (or do not want to consider) the longer perspectives of what they have achieved in their careers and what they could attain in the future. They prize a kind of "continuous present," enjoying their surroundings and the circumstances each new day brings. Other talent traps simply prefer to *avoid* such discussions. Managers may have tried to "fix" them before, and they may have become suspicious and evasive. Or they may have been conditioned to believe that if they don't work, they will receive more time and resources. They may have observed that many managers' natural and intuitive response is to "coax," and they may be waiting for you to start. If so, make it clear that you are reversing that trend.

At this point, the manager has a number of options. One that is often tempting, but which is also the least effective, is to *propose* a goal for the employee, using various coaxing questions, such as

- You'd like to move on into management some day, wouldn't you?
- Wouldn't you like to make "President's Club"?
- Wouldn't you like more income?

Questions like these invite easy answers but little commitment. And, as we have already noted, you can't *give* people a goal. They must determine their own.

A better option is often to simply adjourn the meeting, after asking talent traps whether or not they believe it is important to have some personal and career goals in mind. Suggest that they take some time to think about what they want to accomplish, and ask them to schedule the next meeting to discuss it. In this way, responsibility is left where it belongs—with the individual. It is up to talent traps to determine personal and business goals.

There is no point in discussing strategies or game plans until there is some specific objective to target. Once a talent trap states a goal, however, you have a basis on which to ask strategy questions such as

- What do you think you will need to do to achieve your goal?

When you ask this question, you are asking the employee to *think*. The individual must now develop the game plan or strategy required to reach the goal. The only difference between a dream and a goal is having a process to accomplish it. Depending on the circumstances and the complexity of the goal, the employee may need some time to formulate this process. If so, ask when the plan can be ready, and book a time to review and discuss it. Don't rush the process—it is essential that the talent trap develop his or her own plan or strategy.

Once the employee comes back with a plan, the next step for the coach is to consult on its quality. This consultation is a delicate process in which the coach facilitates the refinement of the plan and encourages further thinking by means of well-chosen questions such as

- What are the strengths of your plan?
- What other options did you consider?

These questions are designed to encourage thinking (and perhaps rethinking) without taking away ownership of the employee's plan.

Once the plan or action steps have been determined, the coach arrives at a critical moment—asking the employee to make a commitment to a specific activity. It's not quite enough to ask

- Will you do it?

Such a question is likely to be answered with the easy "Yes" that comes naturally to a personable, agreeable talent trap.

It is not enough for a talent trap to say "Yes": this is the trap! Instead, ask

- What are you going to do?

Once the employee makes a specific commitment and *then keeps it,* the coach can offer to help. Once the commitment has been fulfilled, and that has been confirmed in the next interview, the coach can take the more constructive approaches that are appropriate for effort eagles and even for golden eagles. After all, talent traps are by definition very competent and often highly qualified. If their effort issues can be resolved, they are capable of being among the best performers.

If the process breaks down, don't try to prop it up by offering support. Until the talent trap is ready to start looking ahead towards activities and efforts, you have no more time to spare. Wind up the meeting by stating the facts: identify (but do not judge) the talent trap's effort issues, and make it clear that you will not take responsibility for those issues.

When a talent trap is prepared to identify his or her specific objective and make a commitment to a new effort, a coach must be equally prepared to accept the commitment. Making and keeping commitments, no matter how disproportionate they may seem to the demands of the job, are essential first steps in developing better effort habits and attitudes. And a talent trap's kept commitments give a coach, finally, something to genuinely reinforce.

Talent Traps: Resources

With some talent traps, coaches never have any real occasion to discuss resources. Talent traps are, by definition, quite skilled and unlikely to be troubled by training issues. They *do* need coaching, mentoring, and support, but until they themselves begin making commitments, they cannot really be coached. The coach only offers resources when a talent trap begins to set specific goals and makes a commitment to the activities that those goals require.

Talent traps must develop their own initiatives. They must put these initiatives into action themselves: you must not take responsibility for, or control of, the process. Talent traps may devise any number of well-thought-out plans, and they can easily make all kinds of admirable resolutions, but you must wait for the actual evidence of effort before you provide reinforcement and support. Responding too soon will make you serve as a kind of cheering section—the first step in a futile coaxing process.

Once the process is started, the coaching strategies used for golden eagles become increasingly appropriate: talent traps who succeed in developing their effort potential can fly high.

Miracle Traps

Miracle traps require the least amount of your time. Weekly development meetings may still be useful, but they may be kept very short, and they may, in serious cases, be discontinued after a very few weeks. In the meeting, describe the facts of the case, identifying in a non-judgmental way the talent and effort issues that you have observed in the miracle trap's performance. But there is no need to repeat this very often. At some point, a showdown will be necessary: let them know that their jobs depend on making a commitment and that it is *their* decision whether or not to do so. Give them an opportunity to remain, and make it clear that they can do so only through their own effort.

Then, *step away*. You cannot change them, and they are not likely to change themselves. In the long run, miracle traps must be dealt with in collaboration with the human resources department. Their presence indicates a problem in the selection process, a problem that can usually only be solved by the termination process.

Be sure, however, to consider how your treatment of miracle traps is perceived by the golden eagles, the effort eagles, and the talent traps. In many management systems, one of the biggest problems is that golden eagles resent the amount of time that managers spend with miracle traps. Strictly reducing the attention you give to the poorest performers will address that problem. But you must ensure that you are not simply seen to be *ignoring* talent and effort issues. You must also make it clear that your attention and efforts are being directed elsewhere. When your people see you working hard, coaching the golden eagles and effort eagles, they will begin to recognize the distinctions that you have made and the responsibilities you have undertaken. And your golden eagles, in particular, will be glad to see your investment in effort eagles: the two groups, sharing a strong work ethic as they do, enjoy the same conditions and work well together.

Coaching the Grid for Maximum ROI

As this chapter has suggested, your managerial time and energy need to be allotted to get the best possible returns—and to ensure that your hard-working people get good returns on their effort, as well as good results.

Miracle traps and talents traps require handling, but not very much of it. Higher-potential effort eagles and high-performing golden eagles deserve careful attention, and they will reward it.

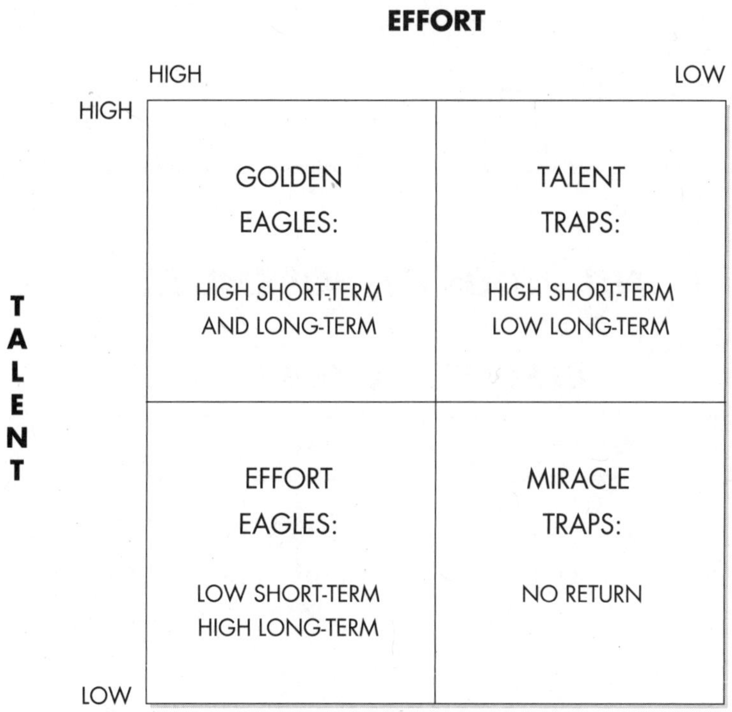

EFFORT

HIGH   LOW

GOLDEN EAGLES: HIGH SHORT-TERM AND LONG-TERM	TALENT TRAPS: HIGH SHORT-TERM LOW LONG-TERM
EFFORT EAGLES: LOW SHORT-TERM HIGH LONG-TERM	MIRACLE TRAPS: NO RETURN

HIGH (top left of vertical axis)

LOW (bottom left of vertical axis)

T
A
L
E
N
T

Figure 11.2
Manager's ROI

CONTINUOUS IMPROVEMENT:

RESULTS + EFFORT

Chapter Twelve

EVOLUTION OF A SELF-MANAGEMENT CULTURE

Practical Priorities

In every coaching activity, whether it is a response to an immediate issue or a structured development meeting, three priorities determine your allocation of time and effort:

- actively supporting strong effort, good performance, and good results
- directly developing eagles through training and coaching
- giving talent traps and miracle traps an opportunity to make and keep commitments

As we have already emphasized, it is best to spend the most time and invest the most energy in your golden eagles and effort eagles. As you evolve, your long-term objective can be to spend nearly all your time with golden eagles and with the effort eagles you are bringing along, while giving talent traps and miracles traps an opportunity to become eagles. That is, by helping effort eagles become golden eagles and by getting commitments from talent traps to make the efforts that will ensure long-term high performance, you will not have anyone else to spend time with. A coaching approach, applied systematically and consistently, will increase the proportion of golden eagles, so that your *first* priority will, eventually, become your *only* priority.

Coaching can be seen to change the proportions of the effort grid. But this is just one part of a larger self-management system, working at every level of the organization, that *reconfigures* the grid. This larger system involves four integrated stages that evolve together:

- selection
- training and developing
- coaching and mentoring
- retaining

These four stages make up a *process* in which the relative proportions of golden eagles, effort eagles, talent traps, and miracle traps are systematically altered.

In this process, every organizational activity is centered on the concept of self-management. During hiring, recruiting, and selection, actively seek out good self-managers and people with strong self-management potential. During training and development, self-management skills are encouraged and reinforced. From the very outset, then, there are fewer talents traps and miracle traps claiming a manager's time and attention, and when effective coaching is used, their numbers will eventually decline. Coaching leverages the strengths of high-ROE golden eagles and effort eagles, while leaving talent traps and miracle traps the option to move up or move on. Day-to-day coaching and a complementary mentoring process tend towards an ideal set of conditions—a "self-management culture" in which only golden eagles and effort eagles are selected, developed, and challenged.

Selection

In some systems, managers may have little or no direct input into the selection process. As a result, they may sometimes feel that performance problems are simply due to *problem performers* and that they would get better results if they could choose their own people. However, they have to work with the existing staff, with the people who are already in place.

This is not really a *coaching* problem. Effort grid analysis is used not only to identify the problematic miracle traps and talent traps but also to show where and how you can use your coaching strategies most effectively. The analogy with sports is useful here. Professional coaches don't choose all the players on the team: their job, instead, is to get good performances from the players with good potential. Good coaches are the ones who get the best out of their players, not the ones who just try to get the best players.

At the organizational level, a self-management system can accelerate the movement towards the ideal by focusing the selection process on effort history and potential. Recruiting, screening, selecting, and hiring must include close attention to a candidate's effort history, as it is the crucial determinant of his or her future performance. Prior to coaching, an effective selection process can screen for self-management potential.

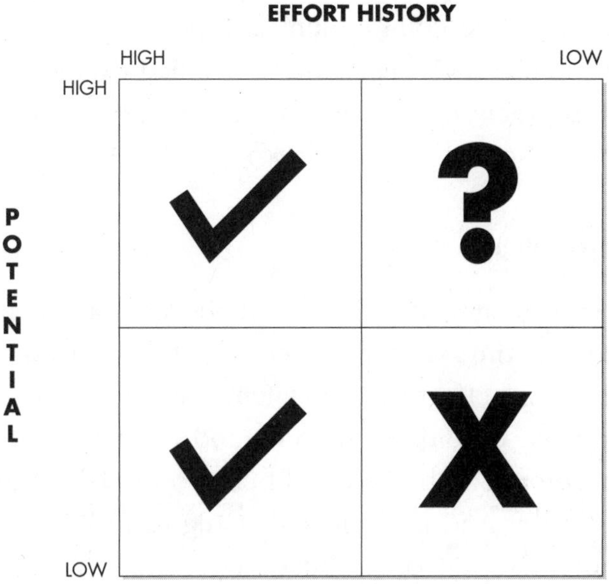

Figure 12.1
Selection

Of course, no selection process is infallible; inevitably, some talent traps, and even some miracle traps, may remain in the picture.

A good selection system uses screening and selection tools to identify prospective hires with high potential *and* high previous levels of effort. To build a self-management culture, the hiring phase can focus on good effort history, and the screening process on qualifications, since it takes effort to capitalize on training, and it is effort that will be coached. The focus on effort history and screening for qualifications represents a divergence from a well-established exclusive emphasis on talent, especially as documented by résumés, certificates, degrees, etc. It also requires that employers resist the very common inclination to follow nothing but their "instincts" or "intuitions" in choosing between prospective employees. Effort history is more difficult to appraise than talent; however, structured behavioral interviews, along with other scientific selection tools, can help gather evidence of the commitment and persistence that will turn potential into results. (For a more detailed examination of these issues, see *Selecting Sales Professionals,* a companion volume in SMG's Golden Eagles Series.)

Training and Development

Selection decisions are often based on the amount of investment, in training time and resources, that a candidate will require. As a result, effort history, talents, and abilities form a prospectus on the candidate. Training and development must consider the *amount* to be invested but also the likely *returns* on the investment. And it is clear that high-effort individuals with high potential will offer the best returns. Training will be more effective and more productive, since it will be directed towards those who have the potential, who can make commitments, and who have the energy to learn and apply new skills and procedures. In the long term, training will not be wasted on those who do not need it (golden eagles and talent traps) and on those who cannot benefit from it (talent traps and miracle traps).

The training phase sustains the evolution of the system, encouraging the proportion of golden eagles and effort eagles to increase. The already low proportion of miracle traps tends to be reduced even further by the "washout" factor: some people will demonstrate that they are simply incapable of performing required activities and will be redirected. Talent traps will not be allowed to waste training and development resources; instead, those will be directed towards promising effort eagles. Appropriate training may be all that an effort eagle needs to join the golden eagles.

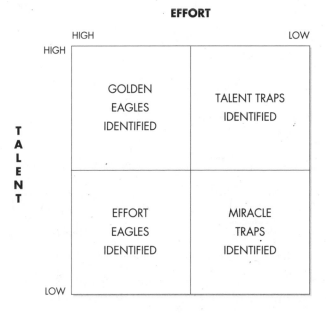

Figure 12.2
Training and Development

Coaching

The job of the coach is to turn effort into performance, and so, indirectly, to achieve results. Training and development focus on potential and effort; coaching on talent and performance.

During the training and development phase, the relative number of talent traps tends to remain the same. In the coaching phase, however, the proportions of the grid may change when talent traps see golden eagles and effort eagles getting your support and attention, and make an effort to develop themselves. A good coach will watch for this effort and reinforce it strongly, since a talented person who makes a serious attempt to develop self-management abilities can become a reliable good performer.

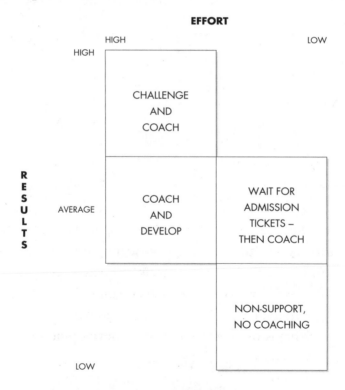

Figure 12.3
Coaching

In this phase, too, any remaining miracle traps must confront their effort and talent issues. A good coach will make *them* responsible for their poor performance and for their continued employment.

Mentoring

In the mentoring phase, the focus is on developing top people. By this point, there is no longer anyone who has to leave. Mentoring builds on the results of good coaching. It requires less direct intervention than the earlier phases of selecting, training, and coaching. The emphasis is on strategizing and setting expectations; golden eagles are supported in their continued growth, effort eagles are encouraged in their self-development into golden eagles, talent traps are offered the opportunity to develop themselves as effort eagles and golden eagles, and miracle traps disappear.

Mentoring can also take a longer perspective on both the organization's goals and the individual's career. Career planning (a kind of long-term coaching) can be used to reinforce effort eagles' development and golden eagles' growth. At regular intervals (quarterly, semi-annually, or annually), an expanded development meeting can be devoted to an employee's career. The basic approach is the same: reviewing performance, commitments, and results; setting goals and specifying commitments for the future; and identifying the required resources. However, career planning questions have a broader scope:

1. How do you feel about what you do?
2. Where do you see your career going?
3. What is the next step in your development?
4. Are you prepared to take it?
5. What help might you need to get there?

Providing a regular opportunity to evaluate career growth

and prospects is a key long-term retention strategy for golden eagles and effort eagles.

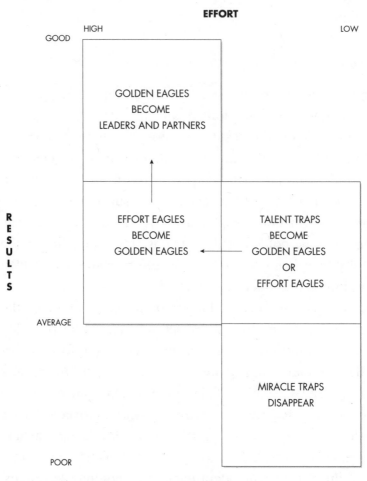

Figure 12.4
Mentoring

A Mature Self-Management Culture

The ideal version of the grid is the product of a coherent system focused on self-management—a "self-management culture."

When selection, training, coaching, and mentoring are all based on identifying and developing self-managers, talent traps and miracle traps drop out of the picture: only effort eagles and golden eagles remain.

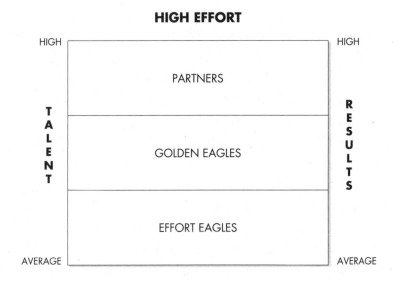

Figure 12.5
The Ultimate Self-Management Culture

In these optimum conditions, the four stages of the process interact, reinforcing one another in an ongoing, self-maintaining system. The system demonstrates a "bubble effect": everyone pushes up. Effort eagles move up to become golden eagles, and golden eagles move up to become partners. Organizational activities are conducted prospectively, with a view to future results and the new possibilities that they will bring.

A self-management culture does not tolerate retrospective inertia. As little time as necessary is spent learning from mistakes. The emphasis, instead, is on the commitments made and kept, the gains accomplished thereby, and the commitments *to be made.* This orientation towards the future ensures a constant renewal of energy and ambition. After all, the past is measured, finite, and done with; there, whatever could have been has been. The future, by contrast, is endless, rich with possibilities, and open to effort. Everything that *could* be can *still* happen— and there our efforts can make a difference.

A self-management culture also prevents the "crisis mode" management that consists of reacting to events and circumstances. The focus is on the detailed processes that connect objectives to results, and both the controllable and the uncontrollable aspects of each step are constantly monitored. As a result, setbacks, obstacles, or shortfalls never really attain the status of a "crisis": they are identified and accommodated before they become critical.

In a self-management culture, then, increasingly high levels of performance are the *natural* product of every organizational activity. Continuous growth occurs as an evolutionary process, not as a result of imposed objectives or artificial initiatives. Golden eagles, as well as effort eagles under development, determine and pursue their own objectives, seeking the satisfaction of not only good results but also good performance. Strong self-reinforcing employees are sure to get good results; better still, however, they are motivated to keep on making efforts and getting more results. In a self-management culture, managers have an opportunity to be the best *they* can be. Released from the requirements, on the one hand, to *control* employees and their activities, and, on the other hand, to *react* to all the unpredictable and uncontrollable aspects of their employees' performance, managers can enjoy the proper responsibilities and satisfactions of their work. As we noted in the introduction, the essential *difficulty* of managing consists in an incongruity between managers' *organizational* responsibility for results and their own *individual* responsibilities. This difficulty disappears when responsibilities are correctly distributed. Self-managing managers, as they coach and mentor their self-managing employees, are always trying to get better results, but they never make the mistake of assuming that they can get those results themselves.

TESTIMONIALS

Here are just a few testimonials from managers and leaders in organizations that have installed the "Managing Effort" coaching system.

"As a result of the training, the individuals got a clear sense of the role of managers and supervisors in improving performance, and in developing a self-managed workforce. I believe the SMG work helped us challenge our approach to performance management. As a direct result of the programs, we reviewed our approach to targeting our resources, ensuring we develop our high performers and deal with underperformance."

**Mike Jeacock,
Executive Director, Service Delivery,
Legal Services Commission,
Government of the United Kingdom**

"The Self Management Group was proactive in their approach to business, listened intently to our needs without pitching, and complemented our existing programs."

**Michelle Manary, VP, HR,
Assiniboine Credit Union**

"The session was very well received by staff...I truly believe we received value for our money."

**Jodie Parmar,
Director, Business & Strategic Innovation,
City of Toronto**

"I saw the 'Managing Effort' program as an opportunity to shift the cultural emphasis within our organization to one focused on execution, accountability, and on driving talent forward…it was the most useful and relevant management training they had ever received."

Lou Rofrano,
Vice-President of Sales Training & Development,
Baxter Health Care Corporation

"Of all the workshops I had taken in my 13 years with Novartis, none had a more profound effect than 'Managing Effort.' I felt as if a big light bulb had gone on and I could see clearly. Instead of facing burnout, 'Managing Effort' allowed me a new outlook and approach to managing my district. The feedback indicated that tenured managers wished they had this workshop early in their management careers."

Cindy Canup,
Associate Director, Management Training & Development,
Novartis Pharmaceutical

"One of the greatest values of the 'Managing Effort' system is the enormous power and sense of personal effectiveness it offers everyone involved in the system—it is perhaps one of the best win/win management systems I had the pleasure of using in my twenty years of professional selling, managing, and training."

Pauline Thomas,
Corporate Training Manager,
ADT Security Services Inc.

"Bob McHardy has conducted 'Managing Effort' sessions with our regional VPs across the country, and the feedback on these sessions has been excellent. Bob and Self Management have a depth of skill and knowledge that allow them to add value to any organization."

Stoney Kudel,
Director, Learning Design,
CIBC

"I took 'Managing Effort' with Schering Plough in May of 2006...that concept changed my whole outlook on what I had been doing up until that point as a manager. Concepts like the 'Admission Ticket' and 'Performance Equation' are just a few areas that helped me regain not only a sense of balance but an excitement about the possibilities in my position that I had not experienced in years. Since April, I've whole-heartedly recommended the class to many of my colleagues, all who have come back with similarly positive experiences."

Curt Gauen,
Senior District Manager,
Schering Plough

"You can't go wrong with Self Management Group. Bob McHardy has been a long-time facilitator at our manager training programs and consistently receives rave reviews from the participants. Why is that? He provides a positive adult learning environment and relevant examples, along with tools they can literally 'take to the streets.'"

Angie Tiedemann,
Manager Development Consultant,
Clarica

"This was one of the best classes I have taken in 32 years. It even out-rated many of the classes I took in my MBA program."

Program Participant,
Schering Plough

"Now that we have the entire management team living and breathing the principles of the 'Managing Effort' system, we will want to roll it out across the country."

Carl DeCoste,
Vice-President, Customer Services,
Philips Medical Systems Canada

"As a new manager, I certainly took away a wealth of great ideas to assist me as I develop in this new role with Baxter. Your presentation style created a great learning environment. I am confident that your seminar will become part of my everyday efforts as a manager."

Beth Flaherty,
Regional Manager,
Baxter Health Care Corporation

"The training was fabulous, by far the best training I have had in years."

Michel Jacques,
Canadian Sales Manager,
ADT Securities

TO LEARN MORE ABOUT THE SELF MANAGEMENT
GROUP, ITS WIDE RANGE OF PROFILING AND
ASSESSMENT PRODUCTS, INDIVIDUAL AND
CORPORATE TRAINING PRODUCTS,
SELF-MANAGEMENT WORKSHOPS, AND ON-LINE
TRAINING COURSES

jmarshall@selfmgmt.com
www.selfmgmt.com
416-746-0444